*What Happens
When We Die*

To Lisa,

Love + blessings,

Echo B.

Also by Echo Bodine

Echoes of the Soul
The Gift
Hands That Heal
The Little Book of True Ghost Stories
Look for the Good and You'll Find God
My Big Book of Healing
A Still, Small Voice

What Happens When We Die

A Psychic's Exploration of Death, Heaven, and the Soul's Journey After Death

Echo Bodine

New World Library
Novato, California

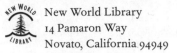

New World Library
14 Pamaron Way
Novato, California 94949

Some material appeared previously in *Echoes of the Soul*.

Pages 10–13: "The Journey Towards Death" by Angela Morrow, RN, copyright © 2013 by Angela Morrow (http://dying.about.com/). Used with permission of About Inc., which can be found online at www.about.com. All rights reserved.

Text design by Tona Pearce Myers

Library of Congress Cataloging-in-Publication Data
Bodine, Echo L.
What happens when we die : a psychic's exploration of death, heaven, and the soul's journey after death / Echo Bodine.
    pages   cm
ISBN 978-1-60868-035-1 (pbk. : alk. paper) — ISBN 978-1-60868-036-8 (ebook)
1. Death—Miscellanea. 2. Spiritualism. 3. Future life. I. Title.
BF1275.D2B63 2013
133.901'3—dc23   2013016539

First printing, October 2013
ISBN 978-1-60868-035-1
Printed in the USA on 100% postconsumer-waste recycled paper

New World Library is proud to be a Gold Certified Environmentally Responsible Publisher. Publisher certification awarded by Green Press Initiative. www.greenpressinitiative.org

10 9 8 7 6 5 4 3 2 1

I dedicate this book to my dear, sweet Mama,
who taught me almost as much about death as she did about life.

❇

Mary Opal Mae McKee Bodine
July 23, 1929–October 4, 2012

Some things are true whether we believe in them or not.

— The angel Seth, in the movie *City of Angels*

Contents

Introduction

*W*hen I was growing up, I was taught that when people die, if they are good they go to a place called heaven, and if they are bad they go to a place called hell, where everyone burns. Heaven was *up*, where Jesus and God live, and hell was *down*, where the devil lives.

Fortunately, in my work as a psychic, spiritual healer, and ghostbuster, my knowledge of heaven and my beliefs about life after death, and death itself, have expanded quite a bit. I'm ever so grateful to all the dying people I've worked with and all the deceased folks I've communicated with over the past forty-seven years.

One of the problems that come with having a more expanded view of death is that I sometimes forget that not everyone sees death as a blessing or as the next step in our existence. For example, a good friend of mine recently called to tell me that he has brain cancer and is going to do chemotherapy and radiation to try to get rid of this very aggressive tumor. Three years ago, this man lost his bride after five short years of marriage. Since her passing, my friend has not been the same happy-go-lucky guy he always was. He has suffered a lot of depression and in many ways has been dead himself. After I hung up from our conversation I started thinking what a great opportunity this was for him to pass on and go be with his wife. I called him back and made the suggestion that maybe he should forget about doing the aggressive chemo and radiation — perhaps he should simply live out his time here as best he can and then go home to heaven and be with her.

My suggestion was met with silence.

On the other hand, in the months leading up to her recent death, my eighty-three-year-old mother, who also had psychic abilities, had no problem talking openly about her dying. She knew that it was coming soon and said she woke every morning "wondering what side of the veil" she was on.

As I said, the voices of the deceased have influenced my understanding. For example, a student of mine told me about being at home one evening and having a vision of her daughter. In the vision, the young woman told her mother she was "okay," and all was dark behind her. My student was confused. The vision was frightening because she had just gotten off the phone with her daughter a half hour before. Her daughter had said she was about to run out to the store to get dinner. But there she was, appearing again to her mother and reassuring her that she was "okay."

As it turns out, the daughter never made it home from the store that night. Her car was found the next morning, upside down in a ravine, the young woman dead.

When a death occurs, I'm usually able to communicate with the person's soul within the first twenty-four hours to see how they're doing. If the soul isn't able to communicate yet, someone from the other side, such as an angel, one of their guides, or a deceased loved one, will let me know how they are. I've learned so much about the dying process and death throughout my work, and I want to share it with you in this book.

❄

Death is a tough subject for most of us to talk about and yet, to state the obvious, it's something every one of us will go through at some point. We need to talk about it. We need to stop making it this dark, scary thing and really take a look at what happens to our body and our soul when we die. It would be beneficial for all of us to learn how to have open discussions with our loved ones when they are in their dying process *and* when we are going through our own dying process. (My mother told me how glad she was that we could talk about her dying because it was something she *needed* to be able to share.)

When I first began writing this book two years ago, I was in the process of losing someone very dear to me, and I hated it. I didn't want his physical body to be so sick. I didn't want to see him waste away to nothing. This man had been a professional basketball player during his prime years. He had been a big man, full of vitality, and the process of his dying from cancer robbed him of all that. There was a growth on his vocal cords that turned his once deep, Barry White voice into a whisper. He had no appetite and walked with a cane so that he wouldn't fall down. The dying process slowly shuts down our physical body, and it's something none of us wants to go through — or watch our loved ones go through.

This book covers a wide range of information about death, beginning with a simple chapter about what the soul is and then a chapter about the stages that the physical body goes through in the dying process. Most of the book explains death and dying from the soul's perspective, and I include lots of stories about people I know who have died and my own experiences communicating with the dead. The final chapter includes suggestions on how to move through grief or comfort someone who is grieving, whether this is due to the loss of a loved one or their own impending death.

Throughout the book I refer to the Elders. These are wise counselors on the other side who have already lived their lives and now spend their time advising our souls about the choices we are making. A wonderful group of loving and accomplished souls, they help us make the wisest decisions for our souls' growth and development.

Angels also help guide us. They too are wise beings, but they are different in that they have never lived here on the earth plane.

Each of us also has spirit guides, souls who have been assigned to us to keep us on our path and help us accomplish the things we set out to do in this lifetime. Unlike the Elders, spirit guides may or may not be finished with their own souls' development; they aren't necessarily all-wise like the Elders and angels. You may have the same guides throughout your life, or your guides may change during your life's major transitions.

I hope this book brings you a great deal of comfort. What I have learned and experienced has not just expanded my perspective but also cemented my belief that life and death are good, and that both make for the fascinating adventure that is our existence.

Everything in these pages is based on actual experiences I've had and is true to the best of my understanding.

CHAPTER ONE

The Soul

*W*ebster's *New World Dictionary* defines the word *soul* as "an entity without material reality, regarded as the spiritual part of a person." The concept of a soul was somewhat elusive to me in my younger years. When I was a child, I used to say a prayer that ended with "if I should die before I wake, I pray the Lord my soul to take." That was the only reference I had about having a soul.

I was in my twenties when I saw my first soul, but I didn't realize what it was. A friend of my mom's, Carol, was hearing noises up in her attic, so Mom and I went to investigate. The world of psychic phenomena was new to us and we really didn't have a clue as to what we were doing, but we gave it our best shot.

There in the attic of Carol's house were four people, but they were transparent. I didn't really understand why they were there or how they could be there. The adult female explained to us that her husband had been an alcoholic when they were living and that he had fallen asleep with a lit cigarette. They and their two kids all perished in a fire. She said he wouldn't let them go to the other side because he was afraid he would be sent to hell. Mom and I had no idea what to do or say to this woman other than that they needed to leave. In response, they went through the wall of the attic and disappeared, but by the time we made it back to our house, Carol was calling to say that the noises were back. We decided then that we needed to learn a lot more about how to handle these situations before we went to any more haunted houses, because we hadn't gotten rid of her ghosts at all and they continued to live in the house with Carol and her family.

When I was twenty-seven, I began my journey of communicating with souls, and it was because of a fourteen-year-old boy who had fallen eighteen feet, had landed on his head, and was comatose. I have told this story before but retell the basics here because it taught me so much — and illustrates so much.

The young man, Dale, was flown from Nebraska up to the University of Minnesota hospital, and his family called me to do healings on him. I had done several healings on his stepmom for heart problems, and that's how they knew to contact me. The doctor had said there was a 10 percent chance that Dale would ever come out of the coma, and the nurse told them that he would probably be a "vegetable" (yes, that's the word they used back then) if he did recover consciousness.

I went to the hospital every day on my lunch break to work on Dale. It was my second or third time doing healings on him when his soul first appeared to me. I was standing over his body, channeling healing to him, when from behind me, I heard a male voice say, "Would you please heal the speech part of my brain? I want to talk again." It was rather startling because there was no one else in the room, but when I heard the same words a second time, I slowly turned around, and there was a young man leaning up against the wall. I was taken aback because I didn't know who he was. On the hospital bed in front of me, Dale's head was covered in bandages, so I didn't know what he looked like. I asked this being who he was, and he very nonchalantly said he was the soul that lived in this body. He reiterated that he really wanted to speak again and asked me if I would please heal the speech part of his brain.

From then on, every day when I went to the hospital I communicated with Dale's soul. He told me which parts of his body were in pain and which parts needed healing. He taught me that when the soul is out of the body, the body experiences very little pain, but when the soul comes back into the body, the pain is intensified. He showed me by going in and out of his body. When his soul was in, his body moved around and breathed more deeply than when he was out. When his soul was out, his body remained very still and his breathing was shallow. To understand this, imagine that the soul is made up of energy and has the same effect on the body as if you put in a fully charged battery; the body becomes stimulated with energy when the soul is in.

Six weeks after I began communicating with his soul, Dale left the University of Minnesota hospital — walking and talking.

Facts about the Soul

I have been working with people's souls for close to fifty years and have learned many facts about them.

- A person's soul looks just like their physical body except the soul looks younger and less stressed and is transparent. Souls appear in clothing.

- The soul is attached to the body by a silver cord, similar to the umbilical cord. The cord is severed at the time of death.
- The soul is our personality, and it lives on after death.
- Each of us has the same soul in every lifetime, and it continues to grow in awareness, wisdom, knowledge, and consciousness.
- The soul goes back and forth between genders; in half of our lifetimes we are male, and in the other half we are female.
- The soul takes many out-of-body journeys when the body is sleeping. This is called astral projection, and you'll be reading about it later in the book.
- When a person is in their dying process, the soul spends much of its time out of the body, preparing for its new life on the other side. During this time, the soul visits with deceased loved ones quite often and reacquaints itself with its new (old) home, heaven. When the person physically dies on this side, they are being born into the other side, *in a sense*. They aren't born as a baby, but they are beginning a new life. We often hear stories about people seeing a white light as they are approaching heaven. What do you suppose a newborn baby is seeing while coming out of the birth canal? The white light, of course.
- Animals have souls too. When my chocolate Lab Jessie died, I was very sad for days, but since his passing I've seen him several times running around the yard like he used to. Yes, our precious pets do have souls

and do go to heaven. They are being cared for on the other side, and you *will* see them again.

Before we dive into the subject of death and life after death, I want to talk about life for a bit. I've written a book called *Echoes of the Soul* that I highly recommend if you would like to take an in-depth look at life, death, and life after death from the soul's perspective. There's a lot of information in there that people have found very helpful, and if I had an extra hundred and sixty pages here, I'd share it all with you, but for the sake of space, I'm going to give you a brief recap.

Our souls are made of energy, and the purpose of our lives here on earth is to develop ourselves to our highest potential. We come from God, and we have to discover what that means. The Bible says that God is perfection and we are made in the image and likeness of God, and the *we* here refers to our soul. But it's one thing to be told we're perfection and another to understand what that means, so we come here to earth, to continually develop ourselves to our highest potential and become even more conscious of our oneness with God and our perfection. At the end of each lifetime, we leave the physical body we have been residing in and go back home to rest up until the next time we come here.

Believe it or not, you have probably died at least *two hundred times* by now, depending on how old a soul you are, so death is "old hat" to your soul. There are different ages of souls and different levels of consciousness. (In my book *Echoes of the Soul*, you can read about the various levels of souls and what each of them means.) To give you an idea of an old soul versus a new soul, Buddha (a very old soul) said it took him 665 lives before he became enlightened (I'm hoping he was a slow learner). The reason you don't remember any of your soul's earlier lives or deaths is that your sanity would be jeopardized if you did. It would be too overwhelming to have recall of all you've been through in your past lives and then have to deal with your current life, so God in His/Her wisdom put a lock on the subconscious mind (the mind of your soul) so that you need to work at getting that information, usually through hypnosis.

Before you came into this lifetime, the Elders drew up a blue-print for your life (also known as your life plan), with or without your help — if you are an older soul, then you may have helped in the planning process, and if you are a younger soul, the Elders planned your life on their own. The Elders have lived all their lifetimes and completely understand what experiences each of us need to further our soul's growth. Remember, the object of each life is to grow and advance in wisdom.

The things you want and need to accomplish in this lifetime are collected in the "life book" of your soul; some gifted psy-chics can access this information for you. The life books of all people are stored in a place called the Akashic Records. I've seen the Akashic Records in many readings, and it's an amazing place that looks like an enormous, very elaborate library.

The family that you were raised in was chosen as the best place for you to experience what you came here to learn — yes, even if you were adopted, lived in an orphanage, or were born into an abusive family. And your life plan indicates when you will die, which the Elders refer to as "graduating." Your astrological chart includes "exit points," or times in your life when your soul could leave and go back home if it felt it had accomplished all it wanted to. Not everyone has multiple exit points; many have just one. I'm going to talk more about this in chapter 4, but the point

I'm making here is that the timing of your death was planned before you were born.

So with that being said, let's take a good, long look at the subject that everyone is afraid to talk about: the shutting down of the physical body.

CHAPTER TWO

Physical Death

There are many ways to die — suddenly, slowly, violently, painlessly, peacefully, terrifyingly, alone, and with family, to name a few. I think it's important to address what's going on physically in death before we look at it from the soul's perspective.

If you are a caregiver of someone in their dying process, or the person dying, you'll want to know what to look for as they, or you, move through this process. Having this information keeps you out of denial, which can be a powerful hindrance for both the dying person and the caregiver. Our body does not want to know that it is dying. It was created to survive all kinds of challenges on the earth plane, so when it comes to actually surrendering to the final step called death, most of us don't want any part of it. As Woody Allen said, "I'm not afraid of death. I just don't want to be there when it happens."

When waiting for a loved one to die, most of us feel absolutely helpless — which we are. This is the final episode of *their* life, and we need to be respectful of this time for them. I can't begin to count the number of people who have emailed me asking why it's taking so long for their loved one to die. Many people try to rush this process along, thinking that sooner would be better for everyone, but there are reasons that the dying process is short for some people and long for others. Rushing the dying process is similar to inducing labor in pregnant women. Births and deaths happen when they are meant to happen, and from the soul's perspective, there is always a reason for the timing and the supposed delay.

When my father was dying, one of the hospice nurses gave me a pamphlet explaining the three stages of death that he may or may not go through. At first I didn't want to look at it because I didn't want to acknowledge that he was really dying — not *my* dad; he would always be here. But as he moved deeper into his dying process, I wanted to understand it so that I could still feel a connection with him.

I recently went online to find a list similar to the one the hospice nurse had given me, and I found a beautiful article called "The Journey Towards Death" by Angela Morrow, RN (see http://dying.about.com/od/thedyingprocess/a/process.htm). I would like to share part of it with you, because it explains the stages of death in such a loving, gentle way.

The Journey Begins:
One to Three Months Prior to Death

As one begins to accept their mortality and realizes that death is approaching, they may begin to withdraw from their surroundings. They are beginning the process of separating from the world and those in it. They may decline visits from friends, neighbors, and even family members. When they do accept visitors, they may be difficult to interact with and care for. They are beginning to contemplate their life and revisit old memories. They may be evaluating how they lived their life and sorting through any regrets. They may also undertake the five tasks of dying. [According to Dr. Ira Byock in his book *The Four Things That Matter Most*, these tasks are: 1. Ask for Forgiveness, 2. Offer Forgiveness, 3. Offer Heartfelt Thanks, 4. Offer Sentiments of Love, and 5. Say Good-bye.]

The dying person may experience reduced appetite and weight loss as the body begins to slow down. The body doesn't need the energy from food that it once did. The dying person may be sleeping more now and not engaging in activities they once enjoyed....The body does a wonderful thing during this time as altered body chemistry produces a mild sense of euphoria. They are neither hungry nor thirsty and are not suffering in any way by not eating. It is an expected part of the journey they have begun.

One to Two Weeks Prior to Death

MENTAL CHANGES

This is the time during the journey that one begins to sleep most of the time. Disorientation is common and altered senses of perception can be expected. One may experience delusions, such as fearing hidden enemies or feeling invincible.

The dying person may also experience hallucinations, sometimes seeing or speaking to people that aren't there. Oftentimes these are people that have already died. Some may see this as the veil being lifted between this life and the next. The person may pick at their sheets and clothing in a state of agitation. Movements and actions may seem aimless and make no sense to others. They are moving further away from life on this earth.

PHYSICAL CHANGES

The body is having a more difficult time maintaining itself. There are signs that the body may show during this time:

- The body temperature lowers by a degree or more.
- The blood pressure lowers.
- The pulse becomes irregular and may slow down or speed up.
- There is increased perspiration.
- Skin color changes as circulation becomes diminished. This is often more noticeable in the lips and nail beds as they become pale and bluish.
- Breathing changes occur, often becoming more rapid and labored. Congestion may also occur, causing a rattling sound and cough.
- Speaking decreases and eventually stops altogether.

Journey's End:
A Couple of Days to Hours Prior to Death

The person is moving closer towards death. There may be a surge of energy as they get nearer. They may want to get out of bed and talk to loved ones, or ask for food after days of no appetite. This surge of energy may be quite a bit less noticeable but is usually used as a dying person's final physical expression before moving on.

The surge of energy is usually short, and the previous signs become more pronounced as death approaches. Breathing becomes more irregular and often slower. "Cheyne-Stokes" breathing, rapid breaths followed by periods of no breathing at all, may occur. Congestion in the airway can increase, causing loud, rattled breathing.

Hands and feet may become blotchy and purplish (mottled). This mottling may slowly work its way up the arms and legs. Lips and nail beds are bluish or purple. The person usually becomes unresponsive and may have their eyes open or semi-open but (is) not seeing their surroundings. It is widely believed that hearing is the last sense to go, so it is recommended that loved ones sit with and talk to the dying during this time.

Eventually, breathing ceases altogether and the heart stops. Death has occurred.

I would like to make a couple of comments about this list from my observations. The first has to do with the dying speaking to deceased family members. If you find this happening, they are *not* hallucinating. Either the family members are there in the room with them, or they are seeing the family members on the other side. The door from our side to the other side, commonly referred to as the veil, is wide open for the dying at this time, and they are much more focused on the other side than this one. Pay attention to the quiet little conversations they are having. It's fascinating when their consciousness is open to both sides of the veil. If you try talking to them, they may not hear you or might become disoriented when they realize that two different people are talking to them at the same time. For example, they may see their deceased sister talking to them while hearing their living sister talking to them, and this can cause agitation or fear. Be aware of this when you're at the bedside of those in this phase of dying.

Several times my dad mentioned one of his war buddies standing near the window in his hospital room, and he would speak to him very softly. What Dad said didn't mean anything to those of us there, but it was obvious from the expression on his face that the communication was comforting to him. We shouldn't interrupt or try to stop this kind of conversation. Also, I could see my grandma hovering over Dad for several days prior to his passing, and she never said anything to us. She was totally focused on Dad, and when he left his body, she took him immediately to the other side.

The other comment I would like to make about Morrow's article has to do with her suggestion of holding the person's hand while they're dying. From the experiences I've had, I liken the last phase of death to the last stage of labor, called transition. This is just before the mother gives birth, and her attention has turned totally inward; she is completely focused on her body and what it's doing. She can easily become agitated with the people around her, yet she wants them there for support. Often the mother wants everyone to stop touching her because all her senses are on high alert. I've seen this with the dying as well.

When I've been in the room with someone who is dying and their loved one is holding their hand, many times I've heard the soul say, "Stop holding my hand — you're distracting me." The soul is working hard to detach itself from the physical body, and when we hold a hand, it keeps the soul focused on the body and makes it harder for the soul to leave. If you want to comfort your dying loved one (or yourself) by holding their hand, keep this in mind. At any sign of distress on their part, let go.

This is not to say that you shouldn't sit by the dying and reassure them that you're there. But observe the process and be sensitive to it. See if you can sense the other souls in the room or the angels who have come for them.

Unfortunately, some people become very uncomfortable if they are in the room of someone dying, and they deal with their discomfort by becoming chatty. The incessant chatter makes it hard to feel or sense what's going on spiritually. If you are in this situation, you may want to ask the chatty person to step outside so you can you have quiet time with your loved one. They may feel relieved. If you are lucky enough not to have one of those people in the room, quiet yourself and stop thinking of the dying person as just a physical body. Remember that a beautiful transition is taking place and try to quiet your thoughts and sense it from a different perspective. Close your eyes and ask God to help you see this event spiritually, to help you feel an inner knowing of the transition.

Over the years many people have told me they could sense angels or deceased relatives in the room when their loved one was dying. The key is to quiet yourself as much as possible and be open to viewing the situation from the perspective of the person dying, not yours.

I had a beautiful experience when I was sitting with a family waiting for their loved one, John, to die. I saw John's deceased parents waiting in the corner, coaxing him out of his body. He could see them and was talking what seemed to be gibberish to them on and off throughout the day. When he took his last breath late that night, I was in the restroom, but I could psychically see his soul come out of his body and take his parents' hands. As John and his parents were moving up and out of the room, in came eight beautiful angels. An angel went and stood by each person in the room. I silently asked an angel why they all were there if John was on his way up, and she said that angels always come to comfort the loved ones. They stayed in the room with the family until after the doctor had pronounced John dead and the family finished making arrangements with a funeral home. When everything in the room was calm, the angels left.

One of the family members who is particularly sensitive asked me if there were angels in the room. She said she could feel a lightness after John left, as if the room had become filled with white light. I was so glad to hear that someone else could feel it also.

One more thing about this transition period: The dying person knows more of what's going on than we do, so don't feel as if you need to explain things to them.

No One Ever Dies Alone

I asked a mortician friend of mine if there were any similarities among the stories he heard from various families, and he said he hears one comment often: people tell him they stayed by the dying person's bedside the whole time except for a quick trip to the bathroom or vending machine, and the person died while they were gone and they felt awful about it. If you happen to step out of the room for a minute and your loved one passes away while you're gone, please don't feel guilty about their "dying alone." *No one ever dies alone.* There are always spirits there to assist the soul on the journey home.

When our dad was in his last days of living, my siblings and I ran downstairs to grab a bite to eat. We had been in his room the whole day, and the nurse said we had time. When we came back into his room, everything was the same except I could feel that something was missing. I looked at all the machines to see if anything had been removed, but they were all still beeping away. Dad was still breathing, yet something was missing. I asked my sister if anything felt strange to her, and she echoed my thoughts and said that it felt like something was missing. Right when she said it, I knew it was my dad's soul. His soul had left while we were gone, yet his body remained breathing. I know for a fact it would have been easier for my dad to leave when we were all out of the room, because he hated saying good-bye! His heart stopped beating the next day.

John, the gentleman I described earlier whose room was visited by eight angels, took a long while to die. During this time, his family called and asked if I would communicate to his soul and find out if he was waiting for something specific. We all assumed it was his son who was out of town, but when I asked John's soul, he said, "No, it isn't his son. He is waiting for the triangle." "A triangle?" I asked. "Triangle," he repeated, and that was all he said. I told his daughter and girlfriend, hoping they would know what it meant, but no one knew. His son made it to the hospital when he got back to town, but John didn't acknowledge his presence at all.

We kept a vigil by his bedside until about 7:00 that evening, when, as if on cue, five of us went out of the room to do something. One of the granddaughters went to get pop for everyone. A couple of people went outside to have a cigarette. One man wanted to check and see if the oil in his truck was leaking, and I ran to the bathroom. Everyone scrambled, except for his daughter, who stood on one side of his bed; his favorite granddaughter, who stood at the end of his bed; and his girlfriend, who stood on the other side of his bed. He opened his eyes, looked at each one of them, said good-bye, and died. A perfect triangle was formed around his bed, with his three favorite people. The rest of us returned to the room right afterward, as his soul was making his way into the white light.

CHAPTER THREE

Getting Death Out in the Open and Celebrating Life

When a loved one passes, we often wish we had asked more questions or had certain conversations with them. What were they like as a kid? What did they love (or hate) about their job? What brought them the most joy? Did they have a favorite book, poem, or piece of music?

Similarly, I've noticed that souls on the other side often wish they had made themselves better understood to their loved ones while they were alive. And those facing a final illness, or simply advanced age, often find it helpful to disburden themselves before they pass on — to explain to those who will outlive them what they believe, what they care most about, why they did this rather than that, and so on. In this chapter, I'll give you a few suggestions for communication and creative expression during the dying process to help the dying as well as those who will be left behind.

Let Them Talk

I've sat with families who were all together because one of their members was dying, and yet no one talked about it. Death is often the elephant in the room that everyone pretends isn't there. This must change, because what ends up happening is that the person who's dying feels very alone in this important time of their life, unable to communicate to their loved ones about what they're going through. We need to change that, for their sake and for ours.

We need to encourage the dying person to talk about what this feels like for them. It may seem awkward at first to get the conversation going, but once they know people are interested in what they're going through, they usually have a lot to say. Their life is coming to an end, and at this time, many people take an inventory of their life. They have memories they want to share, resentments they may be holding on to, happy stories, sad stories, boring stories, exciting stories. They may want to share it all, and they need — and deserve — someone to listen to them.

In my practice as a healer, I work with many clients who know they're dying. Some of them deal with it straight-on by openly sharing their thoughts, feelings, hopes, and dreams, getting their affairs in order, tying up loose ends, and so on. Instead of pretending it's not happening, they embrace this passage of their life. They cherish each day that they have and live it to the fullest. Sure, some clients come for healings hoping to be healed, but others come not to live longer but to feel better and have more energy while they're here. For example, when one of my clients was in her dying process, she invited me over for lunch and showed me all kinds of pictures of herself when she was younger. She reminisced about the men she had loved, the places she had visited, the schools she had attended, and her accomplishments other than raising her children. She had always talked about her children's lives but rarely talked about her own experiences, so it was wonderful to see her open up the way she did.

Unfortunately, most of us don't have this kind of attitude when we find out we're dying. The majority of dying clients I work with are frightened, depressed, and anxious about what's ahead. They go through their dying process in a daze. They don't want to talk about their feelings of anger, fear, or sadness and try to avoid feeling anything. They come for healing for a multitude of reasons other than their actual illness — depression, anxiety, alcoholism, insomnia. These people usually need a bit of coaxing to get them to talk. When I asked him to tell me about his life, one male client said there wasn't anything to talk about, but once I asked *specific* questions — about his childhood, his teen years, his time in the military, how he met his wife, what it was like to become a father, what he did before retirement — he had a whole bucket's worth of stories to tell me. It was fun to watch him get so animated about his life. I could see sadness in him at times but pure joy at other times.

The pre–Baby Boomer generation feels particularly uncomfortable talking about themselves. Many feel it's selfish, so they need a bit of coaxing and reassurance that you'd love to hear about their life. Thinking that this might be the last time you will hear their voice or the wisdom they have to pass on to you will help you get over your own reluctance to face their impending death.

I've been present in many situations where the dying person starts randomly talking about ten different subjects at the same time, jumping from memory to memory, feeling to feeling. All of that is great. It's how their mind is working and how they are able to communicate. Some of it may make you uncomfortable, but remember that this is *their* turn to say it all, so sit on your discomfort and let them get it out.

I was sitting and chitchatting with a dying woman and her two daughters, when the mother suddenly began making amends to her older daughter for disliking her when she was a child. The daughter had never heard her mother talk like this before, so of course she was quite surprised at the words coming out. The dying woman went on to say that she got pregnant at an early age and had to marry the father, who she wasn't in love with, and felt that this daughter had ruined her life. It was interesting, to say the least, to watch the dynamics play out between the three of them. The mother felt relieved to have said all of it, the older daughter was stunned, and the younger daughter kept trying to change the subject and lighten up the conversation because she was uncomfortable with the whole dialogue. Even in a case this extreme, I think the dying person's disburdening is more important than our discomfort. And I suspect that though the elder daughter was sad to hear what her mother had to say, it also probably explained a great deal about their relationship over the years — and it surely helped that relationship grow warmer in the time they had left together.

Getting Rid of Baggage

Another reason I think it's so important to let the dying talk is that they can release old resentments and hurts that they've held on to for years. I had a ninety-year-old client named Mabel who came for healings every week for arthritis. She was a very bitter woman who hated her family of origin, her upbringing, her three ex-husbands, and her children. Every week she would ask me why God wouldn't let her die, and I told her that maybe He was giving her extra time so she could heal her resentments, anger, and hatred and not take it all with her when she died. I also suggested that she start looking at any good that had come from her life experiences. She always said that was "hogwash."

The last session I had with her was kind of sweet. I could see a softening happening in her. She seemed less miserable and said her arthritis was getting better. She usually set up her appointment for the following week before she left, but this time she said she'd call when she needed another one. I sensed that day that I'd never hear from her again, which proved to be true. I prayed that she would be able to make it to heaven peacefully, with less resentment and anger in her heart.

Many people believe that once we get to heaven all will be forgiven and we will be happy all the time, but that's just not reality. Unfortunately, we bring emotional baggage with us when we go back home.

Many years ago, I was the labor coach for a friend of mine, and we were in the delivery room. Over in the corner of the room I saw the soul that was going to live in her baby's body, and he was standing with two spirit helpers and nine suitcases. I silently asked him what the suitcases were for, and he said that they were issues he was bringing into this lifetime to heal. I had never seen anything like that, but I think of it every time I look at a newborn baby in a nursery. I wonder how much baggage they brought in to work on. That's why I think it's especially important to clean up as much of our baggage from our current life as possible before we leave.

HOW TO TALK AND LISTEN TO THE DYING

Recently in my advanced psychic development class, one of my students told me that her cousin was dying of inoperable cancer, and she wondered what she could say to him to get him talking about how he was really doing. She had already asked him several times, and he always gave her a quick reply of "fine." She didn't want to appear nosey and sincerely wanted to know how he was mentally and emotionally and if there was anything she could do for him. My answer was simple: "Ask him what this *feels* like for him. How is he doing emotionally and mentally? Show that you want — and can handle — an honest answer to your question, by being calm and present." Dying people can tell when we're being thoughtful in our questions versus when we're uncomfortable but are asking because we think it's the right thing to do. If we are a little uncomfortable, we may talk a mile a minute or run around fussing over flowers or food. It's better to be still and listen. This also creates space for our intuition to guide us toward good questions to ask.

If the dying person opens up and it seems like they want to talk but aren't sure what to talk about, you can ask them questions like these:

- What are your most memorable times?
- If you could do things over, would you change any-thing?
- What are you most proud of?
- Do you have any regrets?

Ask if they are holding on to resentments, anger, or hatred and speak gently to them about forgiving the persons who hurt them. Do they feel as if they have unfinished business with any-one? Offer to deliver a note to someone if they want to write one. After each story they tell you, ask them what they got out of the experience. What did they learn? Reflecting on and answering this question can be very healing for them. It's better to end the conversations on this kind of positive note.

Remember to ask these questions and listen without judgments. This is *their* story, not yours. They have their own opinions and beliefs about their life experiences, so listen and be willing to learn more about them.

By taking the time to listen sincerely to the stories of a dying person, you are giving them a great gift. Hopefully, when it's your turn to go, others will show you that same loving-kindness.

Please remember that the dying person is in an intense process of wrapping things up from this lifetime. The more they can release their emotional pain, the easier their transition will be. If they can let go of bitterness and regret and arrive home with a clean slate, they will live a more beautiful existence on the other side.

Scrapbooking and Other Ways to Celebrate Your Life or a Loved One's

One Christmas I made a scrapbook for my dad about his life and accomplishments. I put in lots of pictures of him and as much memorabilia as I could find. He was speechless as he went through it. I remember him proudly giving it to my nephew so that he would never forget him, and I've always been glad I took the time to do it.

About fifteen years ago, I lost someone very dear to me. I thought my heart would never heal from the devastation of it. One night I gathered all the mementos I could find from our relationship and started making a scrapbook of everything we had done together. I worked on it a little bit each day and found that the more creative I let myself be, the less the loss stung.

In psychic readings for clients dealing with the impending loss of their own life or the loss of a loved one, my guides often give me images of the client making a scrapbook of their life, doing something creative and constructive to mark the times that were special to them. One of the most common concerns I hear from the deceased is that they're afraid they will be forgotten after they've been gone for a while. We work hard to create a life for ourselves, and when we die it can be hard to let it all go and trust that we will not be forgotten. Leaving behind a scrapbook of our life is a wonderful way to celebrate it — and to leave something special behind for our loved ones to ensure that we will be remembered. Whether you're the person dying or the person who is left behind, I strongly recommend that you take the time to collect your memories in a scrapbook or in another way that makes sense for you (see page 28 for a few other suggestions).

Many people who are in their dying process shut down mentally when they've been told they are dying. They get very depressed and stare at the TV all day, waiting to die. If you're one of those people I'm asking you to shut off that darn TV and use that time instead to make a scrapbook of your life. You're still here. You're still alive. Your mind still works, or you wouldn't be reading this book. Make a scrapbook of *you.*

Entire stores are filled with scrapbooking and archiving materials — and shopping for them might be a fun outing that will lift your spirits. But if you're not able to get out and buy supplies, ask someone to get them for you or order them online and have them delivered.

Make this a celebratory project. If you choose to, get a large scrapbook. Get stickers, glue sticks, and lots of markers, crayons, colored pens, or colored pencils. Gather a bunch of magazines to cut out words and pictures to describe times in your life. I'm going to give you a list of things that you could include, but they are just suggestions. This is *your* book, so do what symbolizes you the best.

- Childhood memories: Favorite toys, holidays and birthdays, special presents you received, special relatives and friends and why they were special, favorite playtimes, books you loved, games you played, childhood pets.
- Teen and high school memories: friends and sweethearts, including your first love.
- College memories: What the times were like back then, your favorite classes or professors, what they looked like, what you looked like, what you loved doing in class.
- Significant love relationships: Pictures and/or memories from each one.
- Divorces or breakups.
- Children and grandchildren.
- Military experience or causes you fought for or believed in.
- Hobbies.
- Careers or jobs.
- Important accomplishments. Hurdles you overcame.
- Dreams and goals never fulfilled.
- Retirement reflections.
- Places you've lived.
- Places you've traveled.
- Things you would like your loved ones to remember about you.
- Things you've never told your loved ones.

- The best times of your life.
- The worst times of your life.
- Significant friends.
- Cars you've driven.
- Things you built or created.
- A section called "Wiping the Slate Clean" listing resentments, people who have hurt you and why, and people you have hurt and why.

OTHER IDEAS FOR CELEBRATING YOUR LIFE

Scrapbooking can be great fun — but you don't have to go that route. The point is to collect your thoughts, beliefs, and memories in a way you'd like others to enjoy. If you're not up for making an elaborate scrapbook, I have a few other suggestions:

- Keep a pen and some paper at hand and jot down notes about the things you'd love to convey. Do *not* worry about being smart or neat or grammatically perfect.
- Assemble photos and other mementos in whatever boxes or bags you have handy.
- Make a recording of your voice or a video. Talk about anything that comes to mind. If you need ideas, see the list of suggestions for the scrapbook contents above. You're making this gift not only for yourself but for your loved ones for many years to come. If you don't have the energy to do this yourself, ask a friend or family member if they will help you with it. It might be a very special time for both of you.

CHAPTER FOUR

Exit Points, the Fence, and the Slide

When I give lectures on dying and life after death, people often ask if the timing of our death is written in stone. The answer is: sometimes. As I mentioned in chapter 1, our astrological charts include what are called exit points. These are important times when our soul can choose to be done with this lifetime. I would guess that many of you reading this have experienced the signs of being at an exit point:

- You feel like you're dying.
- You have death dreams.
- You feel an inner nudge to get your affairs in order.
- You sleep more than usual.
- You feel a desire to get rid of material belongings.

During exit points, the soul is taking an inventory of what it has accomplished so far and is trying to decide, with the help of the Elders on the other side, if it should continue on until the next exit point or if it wants to be done now. This is kind of like graduating from high school and choosing whether or not to go on to college. Do we want to be done with our learning or go on for more and continue our life?

The process usually lasts anywhere from three days to several months, and it can be a very intense time. A wide range of emotions and memories that need healing come to the surface. Exit points are pivotal because if our soul chooses to be done, circumstances need to be set up by the universe for death to occur.

When I was twenty-nine years old, I had a complete hysterectomy. When I woke up from surgery, my dear friend and astrologer Ginny Miller was sitting at the end of my bed and was relieved that I woke up. She ran out to tell the nurses that I was awake, and several nurses quickly came into my room to check on me. One nurse told me that I'd had them all pretty concerned, and I asked her why. She said that today was Saturday and this was the first time I had woken up since my surgery on Tuesday. I asked her why I hadn't woken up before this, and she said they weren't sure and maybe I was given too much anesthesia. When the nurse left the room Ginny told me that I was at a major exit point in my chart and she had been quite worried that I was going to die. My soul obviously had decided to continue to live, but that must have been quite an interesting session on the other side with the Elders for me to have been gone that long! I had no memory of anything that happened during the five days I was gone. Since that time I've been aware of three other exit points in my chart, and obviously my soul continues to choose life.

Not everyone has several exit points. Some people have just one, and in that case the time of their death is "written in stone." If an exit point is more about taking an inventory, the soul usually chooses to stay. When one of my closest friends discovered she had breast cancer, I checked in on her soul and saw that she was at an exit point and needed a lot of coaxing to stay here. Her soul was tired and was feeling as if my friend wasn't doing all that she had hoped to accomplish. She felt stuck in her work and couldn't see any other options. But the universe was being very wise in shaking her up to help her see that she *did* want to continue to live. She had few problems with the chemotherapy and recovered very well. Her work has expanded in ways she didn't think were possible, and she's grateful for all she learned through the cancer experience. Exit points can definitely be thought of as wake-up calls for the soul.

I mentioned that these exit points can be found in our astrology charts, but not all astrologers understand them or how to find them. It isn't a simple matter of one planet conjoining another (or whatever planets do!). If you are interested in knowing about your exit points, seek out an astrologer with this area of expertise.

Having said that, I caution you not to get attached to finding out when you're going to die. When clients ask me when they are going to die, seldom am I able to get that information. On the rare occasions when I do, their soul always asks me not to share it with them because they may sink into a depression and not accomplish the things the soul is hoping they will finish up before they die. The conscious mind thinks it can handle knowing when it's going to die, but truth is, it can't.

The Fence or the Slide

Death is a fascinating subject that tends to confuse us all. I've met clients who were given last rites, only to rally and live for many more years. And I've heard many stories of people who went to the doctor because of an annoying pain and were dead within days of diagnosis. So often, we think we know what's going on and then realize we really don't.

In my work as a clairvoyant, I get my information in the form of pictures and visions. I've come to understand two different visions that I get when I'm working with someone who has been diagnosed with a serious illness. If I get a picture of the person sitting on a fence, I know they are in an exit point trying to decide if they want to stay or go. If I get a picture of them on a slide, I know they are in the dying process, and their whereabouts on the slide tell me how much time they have left. It they are sitting at the top of the slide, I know they still have more time to enjoy their life and get their affairs in order. If they are at the bottom, it is a matter of days before they'll die.

My dear friend Lee died from lung cancer. When he first called to tell me the diagnosis, I checked on his soul and saw that he was sitting at the top of the slide. This was not what I was hoping to see, but at least he still had time before he would die. Each time he called, I could see his soul slowly inching his way down the slide. I desperately wanted to tell him to stop the chemo and radiation that were making him very sick and use what little energy he had left to enjoy his family, but he was determined to live for as long as possible. He knew what I did for a living and never once asked me if I thought he was going to survive, so I kept my visions and opinions to myself.

When the doctors told Lee the treatments were not working and asked him if he wanted to go through another round of chemo, his sister stepped in and told him, "No more." She too was a psychic healer and knew that he was not going to survive the cancer. He accepted what she said and died within a couple of months.

A client emailed me about her seventy-year-old cousin who

was in hospice care. He was no longer taking food or water and was in the final stages of death, according to the hospice staff. They were advising her to "pull the plug" because his quality of life was not very good, and she wanted to know if I could communicate with his soul to find out what he wanted her to do.

From the way she talked, I thought I'd see him at the bottom of the slide, but instead I saw him sitting on a fence, smiling. He told me he was quite content where he was and didn't want anyone doing anything to his body. He was pleased that his cousin cared enough to check on his wishes instead of just pulling the plug. At her request, I asked him several times if he wanted to stay, and he just smiled. He was sizing up the whole situation, trying to determine how strong his body was and if he could live longer. His soul sat on the fence for over a year while his body gained strength. Eventually, he left hospice and moved into a nursing facility, where he lived for several months. He couldn't speak and was quite limited in what he could do, but he didn't care. He loved that he was still alive.

Several months later the woman called me for another check-in with her cousin's soul because his personality had changed. I was excited to see him and find out how he was, but I was surprised to discover that his soul was no longer all smiles. He had a serious look on his face and was three-quarters down the slide. His soul was getting tired of being in a limited body and told me he was finally ready to surrender his body and go home to heaven. I asked him if anything was preventing him from going now, and he said that he was waiting to finish up some important karmic business with someone and then he'd go. My client told me that a week later, an old friend of his who he hadn't seen in months stopped by for a chat, and shortly after his friend left, he passed away.

Denny, a very dear friend of mine, was a happy-go-lucky Irishman who had a million-dollar smile; everyone loved him. He hadn't been feeling very well for a while, and his skin was turning an odd shade of orange. One day while walking around Lake of the Isles in Minneapolis, he collapsed, and a ten-year-old boy on his bike called 911. Denny was rushed to the hospital, where he ended up in intensive care in a coma. They discovered he had diabetes and liver failure from hepatitis C.

About a week later, Denny came out of the coma, and they sent him home with a rigid regime of medications and little hope of finding a donor for a liver transplant. I started channeling healings to him daily to keep his liver from getting worse, while they searched for a donor. The first day I gave him a healing, I was nervous about checking in with his soul. He was so sick that I was sure I was going to see him somewhere on the slide — but instead, his soul was sitting on a fence.

I asked the soul if he had a plan, and he said he wanted to see how much he was going to have to go through before making a decision. Every day when I channeled the healing, I talked to his soul, and emotionally he was quite detached from the experience. It was as if he was thinking of his body like a car: if it was repairable, he'd keep driving it; if it wasn't, he would get rid of it.

About four weeks later, Denny's twenty-five-year-old nephew turned out to be a perfect donor match, and he gave Denny a portion of his liver. I channeled healings to Denny for another couple of weeks while his body was accepting the liver. Interestingly, his soul continued to sit on the fence — he still wasn't ready to commit to his body.

One morning in meditation, I was told that Denny didn't need any more healings, and I checked in on his soul to see if he had made a decision. He was no longer on the fence and had decided to get back involved in his life. He was a documentary filmmaker, and over the next two years he worked on a documentary about the importance of organ transplants. Shortly after the film was finished, he began feeling ill again. He went in for routine tests and found out he had cancer throughout his entire body. The doctors suggested chemo and radiation therapy, and he called me and asked if I would check in on his soul to help him decide if he should do it.

I asked his soul if he would talk to me and tell me what was going on, and I was very surprised to see him sitting almost at the bottom of the slide. Denny was the kind of guy who wanted you to be completely truthful with him, so I told him that it looked as if he had a very short time left and that he should forgo the treatments and just enjoy his family and the time he had left.

Because the body is designed to fight for life, I wasn't surprised to hear him say that he was going to do the chemo, but it sure made me sad. I wanted a better ending for my sweet friend.

He tried chemo once and said, "No more." He died two weeks later and is deeply missed by many.

I'd also like to tell you a fence story about my mom, Mae Bodine. She had emphysema for over fifty years and had many health challenges as a result. One Saturday morning she called my sister, Nikki, and asked her to come over. She said she wasn't feeling quite right. My sister lives six blocks away, so she ran over to see what was up and right away noticed that Mom's lips were blue and she was having a difficult time breathing. They called 911, and as the ambulance was rushing Mom to the hospital, she died. Fortunately, they were able to bring her back to life, and the hospital put her in a medically induced coma while her body got stronger. The nursing staff was honest with us about her chances of survival being very slim.

Unfortunately, I was scheduled to give a talk at a conference in Denver, so I had to leave town for a couple of days. My sister and brothers assured me they would be with her the whole time and call immediately if there was a change. Two days later, I was on the plane flying home, feeling very relieved that I was going to be able to see Mom soon, when suddenly her soul appeared right in front of me. She told me she had been sitting on a fence all week, watching her body struggle to survive. She said she was tired and wondered if it was time for her to be done with this life.

Mom's soul described in detail her upcoming week. She said she would come out of the coma on Sunday. Monday the doctors would do what they considered a routine procedure on her, which would nick one of her lungs and cause an emergency surgery. She would come out of it okay but would be weak for two days. Then on Thursday they would have to take her down for another unexpected surgery. She said she would not survive that one and would be gone by Friday. Her soul was as calm as could be as she laid out these events for me. She expressed no emotion about her death, just stated the facts and then disappeared.

Sunday to Thursday went exactly as she had said it would, and each day I could see her soul sitting on a fence, waiting. Even on the morning of the second surgery, when they discovered a problem with her gall bladder and had to take her into surgery immediately, her soul just sat on the fence. When I tried talking to her soul, she faced the other way as if to say she couldn't or wouldn't talk about it.

During that second surgery, I was an emotional basket case, knowing that she'd said she would not make it through. I hadn't said anything to my sister or brothers and was hoping for a different outcome than the one she'd described. Fortunately, there was.

The doctor came out and told us the surgery had gone just

fine and that she would be up in her room in a couple of hours. The first three days after that surgery, I had no desire to go up and visit her. It felt like her soul was far, far away, and I wanted to wait until I could feel her presence again.

Monday morning my phone rang, and it was Mom. She said she'd had some really bizarre dreams about being on the other side and decided it wasn't time for her to die, so she came back. I didn't know a soul could change its mind like that, but I was very glad hers had!

About five years later, in May 2012, I started having dreams in which I was on the other side with my mom. Night after night we would meet up with old friends of hers, as well as make the acquaintance of many new friends. At first I thought they were just dreams, but they started feeling more real. Even my waking hours were getting a bit strange. I felt like half of me was on the other side and the other half of me was here trying to live in my body. While this was going on, I was having a heck of a time functioning in my day-to-day life. I was forgetting everything. Conversations I had with people one day were completely erased from my memory the next day. I was sleeping a lot more, getting my usual nine hours at night but then taking two-to-three-hour naps in the afternoon. This went on for two to three weeks.

Then one Tuesday morning in June, I called Mom to see how she was feeling, and her breathing sounded as if she had pneumonia. I asked her to please call the nurse downstairs (she lived at an assisted-living place). I felt really panicky about how bad she sounded, so I called both of my brothers and my sister and alerted them to what was going on. Mom called back to say that the nurse, too, thought it sounded like she had pneumonia and had called an ambulance right away. One of my brothers called to say he would meet her at the hospital, so I was able to go to a scheduled chiropractic appointment. On my way there, I suddenly started hearing over and over in my head, "Echo, this is it. Echo, this is it." I called my psychic brother, Michael, and he said he was hearing the same thing in his head.

Michael picked me up when I got home, and we headed to the hospital right away. When we got there we were very surprised to see Mom sitting up in bed, breathing fine, and looking fairly okay and surprised that we were all there. When my brothers went out to talk to the doctors, Mom asked me if I thought she was going to die. I told her what I had kept hearing in my head. She said that that was her sending me very strong thoughts because she was sure she was dying and she wanted me to know. She said right after she sent me those strong thoughts, a voice asked her if she wanted to stay or go, and she said she wanted to stay. Almost immediately, she'd started feeling better.

They kept her overnight but sent her home the next day because she was doing fairly well. The other thing she told me when we were alone was that she was sorry she had been pulling on me so strongly for the past month. She told me she knew it wasn't fair of her to ask me to go to the other side with her all the time but she was afraid to go alone. I told her I had been having very real dreams of us going over there, and she said yes, she knew that — she was having them too. I was very surprised that she was conscious of these "dreams," or out-of-body experiences, and it made me wonder if many of us go to the other side with our loved ones as they are preparing to leave us but aren't aware of it. There is still a lot about death that is a mystery to me.

A few months after this experience with Mom, I had a dream that she had died; I even saw her dead body in her bed. The next scene in the dream was of someone telling me they had moved my mother, and when I looked back at her bed, her body was gone.

The rest of the dream was of my life without Mom. It was eerily real, emotional, and final.

When I woke up, I was sure Mom had died. I'd think about calling her, and a voice would tell me to let her be. I could see her soul out of her body; she was out almost all day. I didn't call her that day, which was unusual for me.

The next day I got a nudge to call her. She sounded good and strong, and when I asked how she was doing, she said, "God called, and we had another talk about whether I was ready to come home. I said, 'Not quite.'"

She told me that she'd then remained out of her body all day. At various times, she'd found herself sitting on a swing with me, her best friend, or someone else in the family who was still alive, so that let Mom know that she was still alive too.

Over the next few months, my sister started getting odd little nudges about Mom. One day she had the feeling that she should make Mom some rutabagas — not something she'd normally do. When she brought them to Mom, Mom told her that just the day before she'd told God she wasn't ready to go until she tasted rutabagas one more time!

One of the misconceptions people have about psychics is that we can see when someone is going to die. I can't tell you how many people have said to me, "Please don't tell me when I'm going to die." As these experiences with my mom show, death is not easy to predict. There may be psychics out there who can pinpoint a person's exact time of death, but I'd say the majority of us can't. That's between our Maker and our soul.

CHAPTER FIVE

The Conscious Mind's Awareness, Acceptance, and Communication about Death

W hen it comes to death, a huge divide separates our soul from our body-mind. As I said in chapter 1, our mind thinks that we are in control of our life, when in fact it's actually our soul's plan that we are living. The body was created to survive, so the mere thought of death does not sit well with the mind. We fight it with everything we've got! I've watched many people go through agonizing treatments to prolong their lives, only to die from the treatments themselves. Modern medicine has yet to find healthy cures for many maladies, and until that happens, many people will continue to suffer in terrible ways in an attempt to beat the odds.

In her pioneering book *On Death and Dying*, Elisabeth Kübler-Ross described the five stages of grief and loss she'd observed in terminally ill patients: denial, bargaining, anger, despair, and acceptance. When we are conscious that we are dying, we go through an awful lot mentally, emotionally, physically, and spiritually in the first four stages, until we finally arrive at the place of peace and accept that the physical body can do nothing more and it is time to let go. My sense is that people are so afraid they'll stop existing once they're dead that they do everything they can to stay alive. One reason I'm writing this book is to assure everyone that we do continue to live on after death, just in a different form. Before dealing with that, let's take a closer look at how conscious we are about dying.

The weeks and months leading up to death vary from soul to soul. I would say one-third of people listen to the promptings of their soul when it's guiding them to get their ducks in a row — that is, get the will notarized, catch up with loved ones, and begin the process of letting go of material possessions. Another third sense the promptings from the soul to get their affairs in order, but they don't want to pay attention, so they ignore the promptings and regret it later, when they get over to the other side and realize they've left their families with a mess on their hands. The last third are people who are so disconnected from their soul that they have no clue that a change is about to take place in their life.

A former student of mine died in his sleep at age fifty-two. Because it was such a sudden event, we assumed he'd had no time to prepare. But his wife told me that in the nine months leading up to his death, he had very methodically visited all his friends and relatives and given each of them things he had borrowed or wanted them to have. He sent letters and emails to the ones he was not able to visit with in person. I was one of the people he contacted, and I remember thinking how nice yet odd it was to get a call from him after ten years, thanking me for being his teacher. I was aware of the finality in his voice when we said our good-byes. He had also gotten all his papers in order and had everything in place by that Monday morning when they found him dead.

After his death, his wife asked me if I thought he had known he was going to die. The answer I got when I tuned in to his soul was that he had *not* been conscious of his impending death but did sense that a big change was coming in his life and intuitively felt guided to get everything organized.

As a healer, I've worked with many clients in their dying process who have wanted to keep the Grim Reaper as far from their door as possible. In some cases, these people have been healed and able to postpone the inevitable. The souls of people whose time was coming to an end have always told me not to tell their conscious mind what the plan was, because they still had things they wanted to accomplish before leaving the earth plane. Their souls were concerned that their body-mind would go into a depression and not tend to the things important to the soul.

One client's soul told me that she wanted to have lunch with all her friends, plant a perennial garden for her husband, and buy a pretty dress in which to be buried. She told me that as soon as she accomplished these three things, she would be gone. This came true, just as she predicted.

When doctors told my fifty-year-old friend Sully she had three weeks to live, she first went through a brief period of anger. *Why is this happening to me? I'm too young to die!* She moved into a place of acceptance *after* asking God if she could have six months to do everything she still wanted to accomplish. That's exactly how the end of her life played out. None of us could believe the strength and stamina Sully had in that six-month period leading up to her death, but even more impressive was how much she and her soul were on the same page about what was happening.

Another dear friend, forty years old, got up one evening after dinner, walked into his daughter's bedroom, and told her how proud he was of her. After this, he went into the kitchen where his wife was washing dishes, kissed her on the forehead, and told her he loved her. Then he walked into their bedroom, lay down on the bed, and died. This was before I learned about talking to souls, so I didn't check in on him and ask if he had known he was dying. My guess is that he was not conscious of what was coming but suddenly felt a deep love for his wife and daughter and had an inner nudge to express it.

Our soul will give us nudges like this all the way through this process. The trick is to listen and act on our sense of silent knowing from within — no matter how strange it seems. Conflict arises when the conscious mind tries to override the promptings of the subconscious. This is when we are tempted to brush off or ignore a nudge.

Until true acceptance takes place in the body, the conscious mind flip-flops back and forth between thinking it's going to live and thinking it's going to die, every day during this process. It is a very chaotic time for the dying person as well as their caregivers. Tempers flare, and crying becomes a part of everyday life; sadness, grief, anger, and despair are all par for the course as one is preparing for death.

If you are going through this process (or if you are caring for a dying loved one), know that all the ups and downs are a normal part of it. Focus on the time you have right in front of you and do the things you love doing. Soon life on earth will be a memory, so continue to make happy ones until you are born into your new life.

If you are getting inner nudges that your time is coming to an end, tell a trusted friend or family member that you need to talk to them about a serious matter. Explain that you don't want them to try to fix it; you simply need to talk it all out with someone. Don't keep it inside to protect those around you. Trying to protect them by keeping them in the dark might actually prolong their grieving process, so be fair to both of you and be honest about what's going on.

For many of us, our intuitive voice pushes us to have these important conversations with our loved ones. For example, when my mom was in her dying process, she had an inner knowing to talk to me about it — all her feelings, thoughts, fears, and anxieties. Consciously, she believed she had lots of time left, but all the same, she felt the nudges.

Another example was my friend Lee. When he finally got to the acceptance part of his journey, we talked openly about his dying. Whenever anyone asked him how he was doing, he would clearly answer, "I'm dying." And, believe it or not, during the time he had left, it was very helpful for all of us to be able to openly communicate that his life was coming to an end. As he got closer to taking his last breath, I could feel his body surrendering and a calmness taking over. He talked about his life and all he had accomplished. Each time I talked to him, I was impressed with how he was navigating the process. It was so refreshing to be able to talk to a dying person about their dying, rather than playing along as someone pretended they were not dying.

If you are in a similar situation with a loved one, check with your intuition about how much to say to them. You'll get that inner gut feeling of *no* if a conversation will not be well received by them, and you'll get a feeling of *yes*, or of a push forward from the universe, when the time is right to have a conversation with them about their death.

CHAPTER SIX

What Is the Soul Doing While the Body Is Shutting Down?

*T*here is no *one* answer to this chapter's question. But there are some aspects of the soul to consider as we look at the various possible answers.

What to Do When the Soul Leaves the Body

The soul is made of energy and can go in and out of the body quickly. If a portion of your soul has stepped out of your body, you will feel physically tired and be mentally spacey — as in the expression "the lights are on, but no one's home." It's a different feeling if your soul is completely out of your body. I hear many stories from people who say they woke up in the middle of the night to go to the bathroom but couldn't open their eyes or move their arms or legs. These people often think they have had a stroke, but they haven't — their souls have simply taken the majority of their energy to go do something important. The best thing to do in this situation is not panic but stay calm and send a thought to your soul that your body needs to get up. It may take a few seconds, depending upon where your soul is and what it's up to, but it will come back.

The soul does many things at night while the body sleeps. It communicates with spirit guides and visits loved ones who live far away, such as in the military or abroad. The soul also visits with deceased loved ones and goes to its favorite places in the world.

You can tell if a person's soul is in or out by observing their breathing and body movements. When the soul is in the body, the body moves around, makes noises, and breathes normally. When the soul is out, the body displays no movement and breathing is shallow. The person makes no noise. They almost appear dead, except that their heart is still beating and so their chest moves.

For those whose death is a long process, the soul goes in and out frequently. When the soul is out, it's best not to try to rouse the person or make them talk. I've been with people at the bedside of their dying loved one who have shaken and tried to wake up the dying person in an attempt to prevent them from dying. The soul can feel someone yanking on its body, and this can be very irritating if the soul is in the midst of doing something important. It's also annoying to the body to be awakened when the soul is out, because the body is missing a large portion of its energy and that makes it difficult to communicate. If you ever find yourself in a situation where it seems as if someone's soul is out of their body, wait until they start to breathe normally again and it becomes obvious that their energy has returned before trying to communicate with them.

The Soul's Activities When the Body Is Physically Dying

The soul does different things during physical death, depending on its age and wisdom. Young souls tend to stay in the body until it takes its last breath, whereas older souls often leave beforehand, especially if the impending death is the result of an impact to the body such as a car accident, plane crash, drowning, or heart attack. As the soul grows in its spiritual understanding and development, it realizes that feeling the impact of physical pain is unnecessary.

I met the soul of a skydiver whose body died after his parachute didn't open. This soul stayed in the body, watching as it fell to the ground and broke into several pieces upon landing. He was a younger soul who hadn't yet learned to leave the body before an accident occurs. Some young souls lack knowledge about death and think that staying with the body will ensure that it will live, but that's not the case. On the other hand, older souls are spiritually aware and know to leave their body before death occurs and head straight to the white light. This skydiver's soul was so intent on staying here on earth that he stayed with his body for hours after it had been taken to the morgue, hoping that the town coroner could put him back together and he could go on living. Later in the evening, his soul even went to the home of the coroner and rousted her out of bed to go to the morgue and attend to him. The coroner was one of my students, and she related this sad story to me when I was visiting her morgue and could feel the presence of the skydiver in one of the drawers.

An older soul can inhabit a young body. I once tuned in to the very old soul of a twelve-year-old boy on life support in a hospital after a skiing accident. The soul had left the room and was already on the other side with his deceased grandparents. This situation showed me that when it is time for a soul to return home, the soul may subconsciously do something to facilitate death and that return. In this case, the young boy had tried skiing an expert hill though he was just learning to ski.

In 1999, after the high school shooting in Columbine, Colorado, I checked in on the souls of the teens who were killed. While one girl immediately went into the light, one boy promptly went to his mother because he knew she would be devastated and he was worried that she might commit suicide. I saw his soul sitting on the side of her bed, trying to comfort her, for days after the shooting. Some souls were in a state of shock, not understanding what had happened or where they were, while other souls understood that this was part of their life plan. Many deceased relatives, particularly grandparents, tried to comfort the souls and encourage them to come over to the other side. Whether death happens suddenly or we linger in our dying process for a while, departed loved ones always show up to help us on our journey home.

When death is not a sudden occurrence and the soul has time to prepare for the ending of its life, the body sleeps more, so that the soul can come and go without disruptions. The soul sends the conscious mind thoughts of things to take care of. The soul listens as family members discuss what's going on. It listens to what the medical team has to say, and throughout the experience, it sends thoughts to loved ones of how it would like things to unfold. When the loved ones are sleeping, the soul talks directly to the loved ones' souls, giving them guidance about what's to come. Those messages come through in dreams, and you can tell the difference between a soul communication and a regular dream because soul dreams feel very real and stay with you throughout the following day.

Even closer to death, souls are very active, as they must let go of a body and a life they have created and, in most cases, lived for many years. Souls regularly go back and forth between heaven and earth, which helps in their letting-go process. They see many of their deceased loved ones eagerly waiting for them to arrive in heaven, and at the same time, they see their living loved ones sitting by their bedside on the earth plane, praying for a miracle. It's an emotional roller coaster on both sides of the veil! (When we are being born, the scene is similar, except things are reversed. During birth, our loved ones on the other side are sad to see us leaving for our new life on earth, whereas our new earth families are ecstatic about our arrival.)

I have two more sweet stories to share with you to help you see the soul's various activities before the person's actual death.

On the morning my minister died, I was in my kitchen baking cookies, when suddenly the curtain fluttered a bit, I felt someone take my hand, and I heard a male voice say, "Thank you." I stopped what I was doing and wondered what in the world had just happened. A moment later the phone rang, and it was a friend calling to tell me that Reverend Clark had just passed away. I had been channeling healing to Reverend Clark for quite a while leading up to this day, but recently his body had taken a sudden turn for the worse. I believe he visited me immediately before going to the other side and took my hand because the healings had given him the energy to accomplish all that was important to him before he passed. I've seen this in many healing clients. Healings may not "save" the earthly life, but they do give the body the energy it needs to accomplish the things that are important to the person's body, mind, and soul.

One Friday evening I felt a strong intuitive nudge to visit my friend Sully, who was in the hospital dying from colon cancer. When I arrived, her soul asked me if I would please rub her feet and then asked me in a very clear, audible voice if I would take her to the other side. I was a bit taken aback by the question because I wasn't certain how she wanted me to do that, but I told her of course I would and to let me know when she was ready to go.

The next morning I was supposed to be up and out of the house by 9:00 AM to do readings at an event, but when I tried waking up at 7:30, I knew that my soul was completely out of my body, on the astral plane — the space between our earth dimension and the other side. I could barely move to call my business partner and tell her I would not be able to make it to the event, but I managed it. I slumped back into bed and slept hard until 4:30 that afternoon. As I was slowly waking up, I heard a voice say, "Go mow the grass."

I was in a total daze and it seemed to take forever for me to regain consciousness, but once I did, I immediately went outside and mowed the grass. As I walked around my yard, my soul slowly came all the way back, as mowing the grass helped to ground my body. When I became fully conscious, I could see clearly what I had been doing all day.

Sully's soul and my soul had met on the astral plane. She took me to all her favorite places. We went up north where she grew up, where she went to school, where she had hung out with her friends. We moved slowly and took it all in. She was very excited to show me all the places that were special to her. Then we made our way into the white light and through the tunnel to the other side. Both she and I were in recovery from alcoholism, and the first person we saw on the other side was our old AA sponsor, Bill M. He came to greet us, and we were both blown away to see him again! Sully was smiling from ear to ear. We had lost many friends to alcoholism, and one by one they came to this meeting place to greet Sully. It was a wonderful experience for both of us, and I felt so grateful to be a part of this reunion.

As I continued to mow the grass, my body began to feel stronger, and I was soon able to clearly remember that the mission was accomplished and Sully was now on the other side with family and friends. Before I had left her, I asked if her body had shut down yet, and she said that she had a strong heart and it would take another day for the process to be done. Twenty-four hours later, she passed away.

"What Is Taking Them So Long to Die?"

As I've said, I often hear this question from family members who have been doing a bedside vigil for days or weeks while their dying loved one is lingering in their process. People often ask me why God won't let the person die and end their misery, but it's not about that. Although it may seem like the person is taking forever to die, the truth is that they need that time for one or several reasons, and it's not our place to question the timing. The dying process is intense for both the body and the soul, and we need to allow dying people to take all the time they need. We need to trust the wisdom of the universe in the timing of everyone's death, no matter how hard it is. Somehow, some way, good will come out of it at some point.

Also, believe it or not, it isn't necessary for us to sit by a dying loved one's side morning, noon, and night. Some people feel that they should do a round-the-clock bedside vigil until their loved one dies, but I want you to know it's really okay with the soul if people are not there at the time of death. In many cases it is easier for the soul to leave when there aren't people sitting around the bed crying and praying for a miracle. The dying person knows you love them whether you're sitting by their bedside or home in your easy chair sending loving thoughts.

In reality, the soul is seldom in the room at the very end of life. In medium readings, people often ask me if the deceased person was okay with the decisions they made regarding their health care at the end. When I ask souls this question, they usually look at me with a blank expression, as if to say they have no recall of what was taking place those last few hours before their death.

I got a call from a woman whose husband seemed to be stuck in his last stage of dying, and she asked me if I would come to the hospital to help him cross over. When I arrived, his soul was nowhere near the hospital, so I waited for him to return. When he did come back, he was agitated about what was going on. His deceased mother was very excited about his soon coming home, but his wife was so deep in grief about his dying that he was very torn about what to do. His body was shot. He wanted nothing to do with it. He was tired of having emphysema and struggling to breathe, but he loved his wife very much and couldn't imagine being without her.

I asked him if there was anything I could do, and he said he didn't know how to disconnect his heart from his wife's heart. He had been with her for forty years and never accepted that this day would actually come. Ultimately I asked him if he was ready to go, and he said he thought he should get on with it. Next I asked his wife if she was ready to let him go. She said, "No, but yes." I then prayed for guidance as to what to do next. I got an image of me cutting the emotional cords between their hearts, and ten seconds later, the man took his last breath and I saw his soul soar toward heaven.

When It's Time to Let Go

On another occasion, a young man called and asked me to come and do healings on his eighty-three-year-old grandfather who had been in a very serious car accident. He said that his grandpa was his whole life and he couldn't live without him. As always, the first thing I did, before finding out all that was wrong with the body, was to locate the soul. I found the grandpa's soul standing in the tunnel (the gateway to the other side), talking with his deceased brother, who was strongly encouraging him to let go of his body and come home with him.

What was interesting was that the grandfather's wife had been killed in the accident and the guides would not let him talk to her. She was already on the other side, and they were keeping her there because they said he needed to make this decision on his own rather than having others make it for him. Grandpa looked anguished about leaving his grandson. I asked him what his plan was, and he pointed out everything that was wrong with his eighty-three-year-old body. He was black-and-blue from head to toe, had broken bones all over, and was developing pneumonia. I told him I would give him some time to talk with his brother, and I would talk to his grandson about what was going on with his soul.

The grandson wanted to hear nothing about how hard this was for his grandpa. He just kept telling me to heal him and make him better. After a few minutes, I checked back in to see what his grandfather was thinking, and he told me that he had made the decision to go home to heaven but would not be leaving for seventeen hours. He said to tell his grandson he was very sorry but just didn't have the energy or desire to continue living in his worn-out body. Seventeen hours later he died.

Most of us, like the young grandson, want to hold our loved ones here so that they won't die and leave us, but when the body is worn-out and the soul needs to move on, the most loving thing we can do is let go and visualize them going to heaven.

CHAPTER SEVEN

What Does It Feel Like to Die?

$\mathcal{S}$ ome years ago a sweet man in his early thirties came to me for healings for a brain tumor. He and his young bride wanted to go on a vacation to get away from hospitals, doctors, chemotherapy, and the worried relatives who had consumed their life for months. He was having problems with vision, walking, and speech, and his energy levels were like a roller-coaster ride. The first time I channeled healing to him, his soul looked very concerned, and I asked him what was the matter. He said he didn't want to talk about anything that was going on or to think about death. He wanted to get healed and get on with his life with the woman he loved.

The healing session produced excellent results. His energy returned, his vision improved, and he was walking stably enough to go on a well-deserved vacation with his wife. A couple of months passed before he called for another healing. All his symptoms had come back and he was bedridden, so I started going to their house for weekly visits.

The tumors had multiplied, but he was holding on to the hope that he would beat the cancer and live to be one hundred. He told me that he was afraid of death and didn't want to die. He was determined to prolong his life as much as possible. When I questioned him about his fear of death, he told me that he was afraid he was going to "do it wrong." He was afraid of taking that last breath and many times asked me to tell him what it was going to feel like.

This fear was coming directly from his soul, which told me that he had probably had a bad death experience in a former life. He may have been like the skydiver who held on until his body hit the ground. He may have been buried alive or had some other kind of traumatic death that his soul hadn't released the emotional memories of yet. If our soul has unresolved emotions from something that happened to us in a past life, those feelings will continue to affect us until we heal them. (I'll talk about healing this kind of fear in a moment.)

When his family called a week or two later to tell me he had passed away, I checked in on his soul to see how it had gone for him. He was so relieved that it was over and that he had finally let go. He told me that if he had known it was going to be as easy as it was, he would have done it a lot sooner and saved himself and his family all that suffering.

I fondly remember a picture that his wife took of him before he died. The room was filled with deceased loved ones and an angel or two. Hazes of human figures appeared all over the picture, making it quite obvious that this young man had not died alone.

Common Fears about Death

The topic of being afraid to die got me thinking, so I went on my Facebook page and asked people if they would share their fears about death with me. Bless their hearts, many people responded, and I want to share the results with you and comment about the most common fears.

Many people said they do not fear death, which is great, but many others did express a variety of fears. The number one fear was leaving their children and never being able to communicate with them again. The second most common was dying a painful death such as in a car crash, and the third highest concern was dying alone. Others' responses included not being able to breathe, not being able to say good-bye to everyone they loved, getting lost in darkness, not finishing what they came here to do, dying young, going to hell, being buried alive, and the unknown. Another big one was people's fear that their faith and beliefs were all wrong and that there was nothing after death. This certainly wasn't a scientific poll, but my guess is that many people besides my Facebook friends share these fears, so I'd like to address the most prevalent ones.

Regarding leaving our children, yes, it can be very difficult to die and leave children behind, *but* if this happens to you, your soul will still be able to communicate with their souls when they are out of their bodies at night. And you'll still be able to see them live their lives; you'll simply be viewing it from the other side. If you die when you have children, there are reasons why this happens, and you may not know these reasons until much later, but you need to trust in the divine timing and order. I checked in on Princess Diana's soul shortly after her death, and she said that her death was necessary because her sons needed to be raised by the monarchy. She was very sad about it and wished things were different, but she had agreed to it when she and the Elders wrote up her life plan. She did as much as she could with the boys before her death, and my hat's off to her for being brave about it and moving on with grace when she died. Prince William commented that he wished his mum could have seen his wedding, and I wished he could have known that she was there in attendance — with the rest of the parents, looking extremely proud.

The second-highest concern about death is how painful it will be, and a few people specifically mentioned not wanting to experience the pain of a car crash. Whenever a news reporter interviews someone who survived a crash, the accident victim always says they have no memory of what happened. As I've already noted, if an accident is coming that will cause the body pain, most souls leave before the impact of the accident. Also, keep in mind that most people who die in hospitals are medicated to the max when they are dying, and that the soul is usually out of the body at the time of death anyway; both of these circumstances result in less pain.

Third on the list was dying alone. The young man with the brain tumor had this fear, which is why someone from his family was always with him. If this is one of your fears about death, keep in mind the picture that his wife took of all the deceased loved ones and angels standing around his bed. Of course, it is possible that you will be physically alone when you die. Your loved ones may step out of the room, or perhaps you won't have any living relatives to sit with you, but I guarantee you, *no one ever dies alone*. You will be surrounded by deceased loved ones, just waiting to take you home to heaven.

The Sensation of Dying

I have a couple of simple suggestions that will give you a sense of how death *feels*. Go to a local costume shop and ask them which of their costumes is heaviest. Put it on and walk around with it. Sit down and lie down in it if they'll let you. Feel what it's like to walk around in it, and observe how encumbered you feel. As you are walking around, getting a full sense of what it feels like, imagine wearing this for fifty, sixty, eighty years. Then take it off and notice how much lighter you feel — that's what the soul feels like when it's released from the body. Some scientists believe the soul weighs two ounces. If this is true, imagine how good it will feel not to be "wearing" your heavy body!

You can also try this: sit back, close your eyes, and take a couple of nice, relaxing breaths. Think of a tree nearby and imagine yourself floating up to one of the branches and sitting down. Imagine the leaves gently blowing and a soft breeze touching your face. Watch the birds and notice how everything seems easy for them. When they want to go somewhere, they just spread their wings and fly. Try to feel how light you are, sitting there on that branch.

Now imagine yourself coming back down to your chair and into your body. Feel the heaviness of your body. The lightness you felt when sitting in the tree is how your soul feels when it leaves the body in death. Because we are still tethered to the body, we aren't able to feel that sense of freedom. In chapter 1, I mentioned that the soul is attached to the body by a silver cord, similar to the umbilical cord. When death occurs, that cord is severed and you don't have to go back to the heaviness of your earth life.

Remember that your soul leaves your body almost every night of your life, so this is not something that the soul is going to get "wrong" — as my client feared. When we are ready to accept our death, our soul simply floats out of our body for the last time.

Healing Your Fears about Death

If you have a pronounced fear of the act of dying, I want you to have an out-loud conversation with your soul, telling him or her to release this fear. Remind your soul that your dread is coming from something in your past and that the tumultuous experience at the root has already happened; *it will never happen again.* If your soul still struggles with this, I recommend seeing a reputable healer who can help your soul get free from this old trauma. If you don't know of any healers in your area, go to my website, www.echobodine.com/healingpenpals, and sign up for the free Healing Pen Pals program. We will assign you a healer who will send healing to your soul every day for fifteen days. This wonderful service has helped thousands of people.

In closing, I would like to share one of the stories that I got from my Facebook poll. Brenda wrote:

Fear of dying? Nope! Probably because I've already been pronounced dead three times. I was born medically dead, and it took the team of doctors and nurses a few tries before I responded. When I was five, I had my tonsils out and, unbeknownst to him, the doctor nicked something. I was bleeding internally, which stopped my heart. As they were wheeling me by the nurses' station, one of them looked down and saw that my face was turning dark blue. They saved me by injecting Adrenalin and pulling me upside down.

The memory of feeling as though I was swimming through thick, gooey mud, trying to get to a clearing, is as clear to me today as it was fifty-three years ago. I suddenly burst out into a space that was warm and inviting. When I woke up later I wanted to go back to the "field," where it was so warm.

Then when I was seven I became very ill with rheumatic fever and was hospitalized on and off for three and a half years. When I was eight (still in the hospital) I had an operation they called an exploratory surgery. They were hoping that if they really got a good look inside me, they might be able to figure out a few of the mysteries they were facing. Once again my heart stopped during the procedure, but this time, for some reason, I had way more control over what I was doing. I had an out-of-body experience that was awesome! It seemed almost as though I were sitting on top of the huge set of lights in the operating room watching everything going on below.

Here's the thing about why I have no fear: they were saying I was dead as I watched them do everything humanly possible to save me. A couple of the nurses were visibly nervous, and one even cried, but I loved what was happening to me up above it all. I could hear *everything*, and I mean *everything* — not just what was being said and going on in the operating room. It was like I could hear raindrops in Ireland, the drums of Africa, the wind, birds, people humming from everywhere, horns beeping, babies cooing, and even things you don't think of as having sounds — like rainbows, stars, and pebbles on the ocean floor. The *most* amazing thing about all I could hear was that nothing was muddled — it all made sense. And I wasn't just hearing everything: all my senses were in overdrive to the complete max. I could also feel everything, smell everything, etc.

Brenda also told me that when she told the doctors and nurses all that she had witnessed while floating above her body in the operating room, they were stunned at her accuracy about what had been said about her and done for her. I hope that reading about Brenda's experiences will help convince you that death is nothing to fear.

CHAPTER EIGHT

Suicide

People commit suicide as a last-ditch attempt to end the physical, mental, and emotional pain they're in. Unfortunately, though, the emotional and mental pain is in the soul as well. So although they commit suicide to get rid of the pain, they inevitably take the pain with them to the other side. I've worked with many suicide souls in my work as a ghostbuster (which I chronicle in my book *The Little Book of True Ghost Stories*), and it always saddens me to see how much pain they're still in after they take their life.

I grew up with depression and became an alcoholic in my early twenties. Drinking alcohol is a stupid way to cope with depression, but that's what I did. The thought of suicide was always in the back of my mind. It felt good to know there was a way out of the pain if it ever got too bad. One night I sat down with a glass of water and a bottle of Valium intending to end my life. Instead, I was shown a vision of complete darkness. A voice told me that this is what I would find if I went through with it. That darkness looked so lonely, and I was angry that this wasn't the positive solution I was looking for. Shortly afterward, I joined Alcoholics Anonymous, and I have found many gifted therapists and doctors over the years who have helped me heal the depression.

The pain in our souls is an accumulation of unresolved issues from previous lives, all waiting to be addressed. Remember the story of the soul in the delivery room with his nine suitcases of issues he was bringing in to heal? That's what happens when we leave a life full of unresolved mental and emotional pain: we bring it with us into our next life with the hopes of finally healing it.

Do People Who Commit Suicide Go to Heaven?

The darkness that I saw in my vision is not necessarily where suicide souls go. I think it was showing me what my mental state would be if I took my own life. Some religions say that those who commit suicide are not allowed into heaven until their allotted time, until the time they were "meant" to die, but that's not true. God welcomes all of us home whenever and however we die.

Earthbound suicide souls stay here by choice. Most of them are embarrassed that they chose suicide instead of finishing what they came here to do. Some are afraid they are going to get sent to hell for taking their life, and others believe they don't deserve to go to heaven and don't even make the attempt. Their spirit guides try to convince them to come home; sometimes they succeed, and sometimes they don't. The guides can't force anyone against their will, *but* if a person dies from an overdose and the soul is unconscious, the guides will take that soul over to the other side and put it in a hospital where it will get the help it needs when it wakes up (more on this in chapter 11). Not all overdoses are meant to be suicides, and some souls are in deep grief when they realize their life is over because they took too many drugs. Fortunately, there are wonderful caregivers in heaven who will work with them as they go through their grieving process.

When the media reported the accidental suicide of actor David Carradine in 2009, I checked in on his soul to see how he was doing. He was having a heck of a time figuring out what was going on. Almost two full days passed before he realized that he wasn't dreaming and he had accidentally killed himself. His soul would not leave the closet where they found his body because he kept thinking that if he would just wake up from this terrible dream he was having, he'd be fine. For two days he was in complete denial that his life had ended. I heard him say several times, "If I could just wake up," but of course his physical body couldn't.

A dear friend who I met in recovery also suffered from severe bouts of depression most of his life and tried many things to get better. Finally, one night in desperation he took a huge overdose of pills, fully intending to end his life, but some friends found him and rushed him to the hospital. This was particularly tough for me because we had become very close and I had thought he was getting better. He ended up on life support, and his soul came to me; it was very clear that he knew what he had done and that he had intended to end his life. He asked me to please call the people who were making the decisions about what to do with him and tell them he wanted them to pull the plug. He was angry that they had interfered and he just wanted to get on with life on the other side.

I prayed for guidance on how to approach his friends because I wasn't sure how they would take this news. Fortunately, about half an hour after I said that prayer, one of his friends called and asked if I would check in with him to find out what he wanted them to do, and I was able to relate his message to them. They pulled the plug that night, and he died shortly afterward.

I've checked in on him over the years, and he seems to be doing fairly well, though he does have a "suicide aura"; this is the energy of unfinished business and sadness, and I've seen it in other suicide souls as well. I've asked him a couple of times if he regretted ending his life. At first he always hesitates, but then he says no, it was what he needed to do.

Not everyone is as clearheaded as he was. I had a client named Cathy who struggled with depression, alcohol, and drugs. She had been in treatment at least half a dozen times and just could not pull it together. She had tried suicide a couple of times but was found before it was too late. Finally her family had her committed to a long-term treatment facility, and everyone was hopeful that she might make it this time. She was a master manipulator who could sell ice to an Eskimo, so I wasn't surprised to hear that she had convinced an intern to let her go outside for a walk one sunny Saturday afternoon. She walked up to the roof of the building and jumped to her death. She had been determined to end it all, and I would guess this was not only for her sake but for her family's as well.

When I got the call about her death, I immediately tried tuning in to her soul to see how she was. She was so out of it that I could not communicate with her at all. Her soul was an emotional mess, and I was very sad to see that the peace she had hoped to find totally eluded her. I've tried a few times to check and see how she's doing, but I've always gotten static, which has told me to leave it alone and give her the space she needs.

Suicide Souls' Biggest Regret

The biggest regret I hear from suicide souls is that they wanted relief — from the bill collectors, the mortgage company, the pain in their body, their depression, addiction, a broken heart, nagging parents, the bullies in their life — but it never occurred to them how permanent suicide is. They get over to the other side and have no more bill collectors or threats of foreclosure, their broken heart starts to mend, the bullies no longer matter — and then they feel ready to come back.

That's when it hits them that death is permanent. Death is not just a two-month reprieve from the hassles of life. We can't put our life on pause for a little bit while things calm down. When we take our own life, we are done, finished. This body will never exist again.

That's why it is so fortunate that many suicide attempts don't end in death. For example, a man came to me for healings after trying to take his own life. He had planned everything very carefully, making sure to take the overdose of pills when his roommate would be gone for several hours.

He wrote a note to his family telling them how sorry he was but that he just couldn't live with his depression anymore. He got all his affairs in order and lay down with a stomach full of pills, looking forward to meeting St. Peter at the gates of heaven. Instead he woke up in an emergency room. His roommate had forgotten something at home and had gone back to get it.

This would-be suicide told me he had made his job his everything and had forgotten that other things were important too. All he did was work, work, work to pay the bills, and he felt like he still couldn't get ahead. He just wanted a break from it all, and when it really hit him that he had attempted suicide, it totally freaked him out. He said he was going to make two major changes in his life. One was cutting back his hours at work, and the second was doing whatever he needed to do to heal the depression. He said that over the years he had done some therapy and taken medication on and off, but he had never stuck with any of it for very long, and that was going to change.

He came for a few healing sessions and I noticed that a gradual change was taking place. Little by little he was becoming a happier person. He changed his priorities and started seeing all kinds of possibilities for himself. He was a wonderful guy who had a lot to offer this world. I'm so glad his roommate forgot something at home that fateful day!

For those of you suffering from depression, I really want to caution you about ending your life to stop that pain. The feeling of hopelessness is in your soul, and chances are you came here this lifetime to heal it. Please talk to your doctor about getting on a good medication to balance out the chemicals in your body. If you are on meds already and they're not working, *please* tell your doctor. Doctors aren't mind readers and will only know what's going on if you tell them. Then find a very competent therapist to work with who understands depression and doesn't let you tell the same old stories over and over. You need someone who can get to the heart of your pain and help you heal it.

You may need to try more than one therapist. I've had some who would let me sit and talk, talk, talk about how awful my life was. They were happy to take my money. Then I found someone who in our first visit told me she wasn't out to make her house payments off my depression. She wanted to get me healed and back to my life. She wasn't interested in hearing my same old stories. She wanted to know the feelings behind these stories, and that's when I truly began healing. She changed the cycle of depression for me, and all the hard work was well worth it.

I also suggest getting a copy of *My Big Book of Healing*, which I wrote to help people recover from all sorts of challenges, including depression. Reading through it will help you identify what issues you need to work on.

If you know someone who has recently committed suicide, try communicating with their soul to help them heal. They may be very confused, and your guidance can be very helpful. Here are some guidelines for reaching out to and connecting with them:

- Do your best to make contact with them by saying their name out loud.
- Tell them to go to the white light. Assure them that they will find the help they need there, not judgment.
- Let them know that you are okay, which will put their mind at ease, and that you forgive them. It may take a while before you can honestly say this, but when that time comes and you have forgiven them, be sure to tell them so.
- Later on, when they've been on the other side for a while, you can tell them how you feel about their death, but in the beginning just focus on reassuring them that they will be welcomed home if they follow the white light.

CHAPTER NINE

The Soul's Journey from Death to the Funeral and Beyond

What we do in the interim between our death and our funeral varies from soul to soul. It has much to do with our beliefs and expectations about heaven and death. Older souls usually go right to heaven because they've been through this many times and know how it works, and then they come back for the funeral. Very young souls often linger here on earth. They may stay stuck in anger, hatred, or grief for quite a while until they are ready to move on. If they were murdered, they might linger here on earth to seek revenge for their death. Other souls stay here in the interim period because they're very concerned about their families, especially children, or about their body. Others stick around because they're confused about having died. I'll give you a few examples.

Recently a dear friend of mine suddenly lost his forty-six-year-old sister; she lay down for a nap and never woke up. I tuned in to her soul as soon as he contacted me, and she was extremely fragile and quite confused about what was going on. She wanted to know why she had died and if she had done something wrong and was being punished for it. Her guides asked me to have her brother talk to her to assure her that she hadn't done anything wrong and it was simply time for her to be done with her life. They also asked him to encourage her to go toward the light.

For the next five days I checked in on her daily because my friend was very concerned about her. What I saw when I tuned in to her was similar to a caterpillar turning into a butterfly. It was *very important* that no one on this side pull on her energy by pleading with her to come back and be with them. The guides were also adamant that the family wait for at least five days to have the funeral so that she would be strong enough to attend it. The family heeded the request.

As I've already stated, I can see the soul clearly for the first couple of days after the body's death. But usually by the third day, the veil is closed and the soul is off-limits to those of us here because it is being taken care of on the other side. It is in a nurturing/resting place and usually isn't seen again until the funeral.

On the day Michael Jackson died, I tuned in to his soul and was pleasantly surprised to see that he was very alert and didn't seem at all shocked that he had died. His death felt meant to be. I was surprised that he was so accepting of his death because in my mind he was still a young man and had so much more to experience with his children, his family, and his creative gifts, but his soul was peaceful and relieved. As much as I wished he hadn't died, I felt happy for him. I saw how evolved his soul was and how tough life had been for him here. He was grateful that his life was over because few people outside his family had really understood who he was.

Two days after Jackson's death, I again checked in to see how he was doing and this time was delighted to see him sitting in an outdoor setting with Elvis Presley! They were sitting on big stones in front of a rushing creek. There was lush greenery in the background, and the energy surrounding both of them was private, peaceful, and powerful. They were talking like old soul mates who had both come to earth to accomplish similar things and had much to discuss. The next time I checked in on Jackson, the veil was closed and there was a very calm sense about him; I felt that he was being well protected from the crowds of souls on the other side who wanted to see him.

He attended his funeral and was overwhelmed with gratitude for all the people who showed up. He felt truly humbled by it. His funeral and all the attention he got in the end helped to heal the hole in his heart that was created when people had falsely accused him. I was glad to see he was happy about his children being with his mother and that he was confident they would go to school, have friends, be surrounded by family, and not have the pressures on them that he had as a child. He felt that his mother would do right by them and that they would have a more normal upbringing with her than they would have had with him.

Several years ago I did a TV shoot with Farrah Fawcett, and when I heard she had passed away (on the same day as Michael Jackson), I checked in on her soul to see how she was. She was surrounded by her mother and all the female relatives on her mother's side. They created a circle around her and took her sleeping soul to the other side. They stayed with her all week leading up to her funeral and shielded her from the grief energy that people on this side were unintentionally sending to her.

I encountered some lingering souls when I investigated a possible ghost situation at a funeral home a couple of years ago. The home's director said that he heard strange noises — banging on the walls, things falling, and sounds of tools being used — coming from one of the rooms in the basement, and he wanted me to investigate. I sensed that there was more than one spirit lingering in the building, so I told him I wanted to check out the whole place.

While walking through the rooms on the main floor, I came upon the soul of a man whose funeral had just taken place that morning. He was sitting where the casket had been, looking very sad. I asked him why he was there, and he said that he just wanted "to stay here until the procedure at 2 o'clock" and that he would go to the light after that. I asked the funeral director if there was a procedure being done on him at 2, and he said that the body was scheduled to be cremated at noon. No sooner had he said this than his phone rang, and it was someone from the crematorium telling him that they couldn't get to this man until 2 o'clock. I told the man's soul how sorry I was that he was going through this and that he would find great peace on the other side, but I also knew that he needed to do his own grieving for the loss of his body. Then I said good-bye to the man and headed downstairs.

As I was walking down the hall in the basement, I could psychically see a female soul sitting by the head of a body inside one of the prep rooms. I asked her what she was doing there, and she said that she wanted to make sure they did her hair correctly and that she didn't want to be with her family right now because they were all fighting.

I told the funeral director about the woman, and he had a good chuckle. He said he had known her most of his life and she had always been concerned about her hair! He also said that, yes, her family was fighting and he could understand why she didn't want to go and hang out with them. However, the strange noises weren't coming from the prep room where she was, so I kept looking.

In the maintenance room of the funeral home, I found a male spirit. He told me he was the former janitor and had taken care of the building his whole adult life. He said he knew about the white light but wanted to stay here and continue to take care of the place. He was an example of an earthbound spirit or ghost — a soul that chooses to remain on the earth plane after death, rather than going on to the other side. The director confirmed that the sounds were coming from the janitor's room and that they started shortly after he died. Although the janitor insisted that he still wasn't ready to move on, he said he would stop making noise.

The Funeral

People often ask me if we attend our own funerals, and the answer is a resounding *yes* — the vast majority of the time our soul does attend, with only a couple of rare exceptions, which I'll explain at the end of this section. I can't ever remember attending a funeral when the soul was not present. I've seen whole families from the other side escort their loved one to their funeral; it's an all-out, multigenerational family affair.

I recently went to my friend Denny's wake. This is the man who had a liver transplant and then died from cancer a couple of years later. Denny was a very outgoing guy with a fun sense of humor and a drop-dead smile. He always lit up a room, no matter what was going on. I was a bit surprised that he wasn't there when I first arrived. I even walked around the place to see if he was in a different room, because for Denny to miss his wake would have been too weird. I gave up looking and was talking to some mutual friends about the documentary Denny had made, when suddenly I heard his voice in my head say, "What the hell?" I literally laughed out loud because it was so obvious that he was there. I looked around the room, and he was standing at the head of the coffin looking down at his body.

I have no idea what the morticians did when preparing his body, but he looked awful. His normally thin face was bloated. He had little slits for eyes and a mouth. It was very disconcerting to look at him. And there was his soul, looking down at himself and asking, "What the hell?"

I watched as he walked up to each person in attendance to hear what they were saying. He listened intently to everyone who arrived. It was all quite emotional for him, and at times he would leave the room.

I was not able to attend his funeral the next day, but my psychic brother, Michael, who was one of the pallbearers, assured me that it was a wonderful Catholic-Irish affair and that Denny was there the whole time.

Another memorable funeral I attended was that of my mom's boyfriend Jerry. When the services were over and we were at the luncheon, Jerry stood right next to me and said, "Ec, it isn't fair. This is my funeral, and I don't get to eat any of the food." Two things he was known for were his love of food and his great sense of humor. He was taking in all the smells and hopping from table to table to listen to his friends reminisce about him. He was so happy that day, seeing all his friends and family together in the same room. He didn't even mind the "rented" priest they had found to do his eulogy, even though he was totally off base about Jerry and his life.

The one thing that stands out the most about this funeral was that Jerry had requested they play the song "When the Saints Go Marching In," and when they turned on that music, his soul was dancing in the aisle with a huge grin on his face. He had been in poor health for a long time, so it was great to see him looking healthy again, dancing down the aisle, surrounded by loved ones. It was a great way to end a funeral service.

In rare cases, souls don't attend their funerals, for one of two main reasons. First, it's too emotional. The soul is having a very tough time accepting the death and therefore is itself heavily grieving. Second, it is too weak to attend. This can happen if the person had a long death process and clung to life as long as possible. The physical body may have taken as much energy as it could from the soul, and the soul then needs to build its energy back up. This replenishment comes through resting and being nurtured — which the soul does plenty of on the other side.

One of the best things about the other side is how laid-back things are. If the soul doesn't attend the funeral, whenever it feels ready later it can view the funeral, as if watching a movie. The funeral is also part of the "life review" souls do at a later time. This is when the soul sits with the Elders and goes through its Akashic records to look over the original blueprint for its recent lifetime and assess the progress it made. What had it hoped to accomplish, and did it do those things? How much did the soul grow? Did the person make amends to the people they hurt? What new karma did they create for themselves through their good and not-so-good deeds?

After the Funeral

I have noticed that souls tend to do a disappearing act right after the funeral and don't show up again until weeks or months later. One day I was out mowing the grass and wondering about this, and into my head came these words from Lilli, one of my angel guides: "It's best not to go back to the old neighborhood right after moving away." Then a memory came to me of when I was fourteen and we moved from a neighborhood we had lived in most of my life to a brand-new suburb, away from all my friends.

I hated moving, but my parents said it was the opportunity of a lifetime and the timing was perfect. They told us we could go back and see our old friends anytime we wanted, but after the initial move, it became pretty obvious that our parents wanted us to concentrate on the new neighborhood and make friends with the kids there.

It didn't seem fair to me at the time. I really missed my old life and wanted to be with the only friends I had ever known, but my parents kept nudging us to focus on the new neighborhood and on making new friends. After a while the old neighborhood seemed far away, and I could see why it was important to give the new home and new friends a chance to be as special as the old neighborhood had been. It's been fifty years since I lived in that old neighborhood, and I go back once in a while to visit and reminisce. I have wonderful memories from both of my childhood homes, and I'm grateful to my parents for teaching us how to move on.

As I continued to mow the grass, I had an "aha" moment in which I understood why the Elders are always encouraging deceased souls to move on, into their new life. It's part of the souls' growth to move on. The Elders aren't keeping them from their loved ones on this side, but there was a reason (maybe many) why they died before their loved ones and the loved ones are left to live their lives without them. And the sooner the soul stops visiting the old neighborhood and moves on, the faster the soul will grow.

Many people ask me why they haven't felt their deceased loved one after the funeral, and I understand now that it's because souls need to take a "time-out" from earth before coming back to visit. They need to disengage from the old neighborhood so that they can go through their own grieving process for their former life and loved ones. After they've been on the other side for a while and have detached themselves emotionally from their previous life, they start making their presence known once again.

CHAPTER TEN

When Children Die

One of the lessons I've learned over and over in my work is to never take anyone's life for granted. Unfortunately, we do this all the time. We settle into our routines, we're busy, and for some odd reason we think that life will never change and the people we care about will be around forever. But that's not why we've come here. Our soul chose this life on earth to have some very specific experiences, and when we've accomplished those, our soul goes back home. Our time here isn't infinite, and neither is that of the other people in our lives.

Often when a child dies, someone says, "A parent should never have to bury their child." This always gives me pause. I've never once seen a child be born with a long-lifetime guarantee. Yes, it would be ideal if no parent had to bury a child, but that's just not how life here works.

I wanted to write a chapter about the death of children for two reasons. First, I want to impress upon people that when you give birth to a child, the child comes in with a life plan, a blueprint of the things they want and need to experience. They chose you as the parents and family in which to learn and have their life experiences. This does not mean they have a long life planned.

I've heard parents say, "She'll never go to prom or walk down the aisle." But I can assure you that if those experiences were important to that child's soul, the child would have stayed and had them. The same holds true for sons or daughters killed in the military. As hard as it may be for us to accept, dying in combat was part of their plan. They wanted to experience the military and learn as much as they could from it, and then they were done.

This all may sound cold and uncaring, and I don't mean it to *at all*. I have to remind *myself* from time to time when I hear of a child's death that this is part of their life plan, and those of their family members. Recently I saw a story on the news of a fifteen-year-old girl who was sitting in the park with her boyfriend waiting for the bus, when a man lost control of his legs and sped his car across the park and killed her. I thought about that poor family for days afterward. It's just plain horrible when these tragedies happen.

In the past month here in the Twin Cities, two little boys, ages three and five, were killed in separate gang-related incidents. One of the reasons a soul may choose to live a short life and then die by this kind of violence is to wake up the community and make change happen. On a similar note, three children drowned last summer. This kind of accident always makes me wonder what the souls hoped to accomplish from their short lives and death. I come back to the fact that it is not unusual for seemingly senseless deaths to have been chosen by a soul to somehow positively impact a community.

In chapter 6, I mentioned the twelve-year-old boy who died while skiing, but I didn't tell you about the year leading up to his death. Shortly after his eleventh birthday, his mom, my friend

Melody Beattie, told me she had a strong sense that she should spend as much time with her son as possible, and we both figured it was because she had been traveling a lot for work. The whole following year was magical for both of them. She stuck to her commitment in spite of work-related demands and spent a lot of time doing all the things her son wanted to do. For his twelfth birthday he asked her for a very special knife set. I remember her saying it seemed crazy to buy a twelve-year-old such an expensive gift, but her gut was telling her to go ahead. So she bought it for him, and he was thrilled beyond words.

Three days after his birthday, his sister took him skiing, and he died on the slopes. As incredibly tragic as his death was, good eventually came out of it, but it took a while for the family to see it. Melody is a successful author, and after she got through the first year of horrendous grief, she wrote a book called *The Lessons of Love* that has helped millions of people who have lost a child.

Six years after this boy's death, his father lost his fight with alcohol and drug addiction, and I could tell how important it was for him to see his son as soon as he went over to the other side. It was a blessed family reunion for those on the other side, though it was a tremendously difficult time for us on this side.

My second reason for writing this chapter is to let you know that sometimes the children we lose come back to us at a later birth. For example, about a year ago, a couple from India emailed me about the loss of their son, who had died shortly after he was born. They were extremely distraught over his death because they had tried for years to have a child and all the woman's earlier pregnancies had ended in miscarriages. I opened up psychically and asked if the soul of the boy would talk to me. Within seconds, his soul came and told me that he would be coming back to his parents shortly. He said the body he had been born into had some physical problems, which the parents later confirmed, and he said he wanted a stronger, healthier body. He was quite calm about the whole experience, for he knew that it was just a matter of time before he'd be back. A month ago, the couple emailed me to say that they now have a very healthy baby boy, and I was very glad to hear he had been reborn.

This next tragic story had a happy ending as well. A few years ago a friend of mine was on her way to daycare to pick up her four-month-old daughter. The whole way there, she was following an ambulance and said a prayer for whoever might be inside. When the ambulance pulled into the parking lot at the daycare, her heart sank as her mind raced to all the children inside, wondering who might need help.

Unfortunately, it was her daughter — she had died and they were not able to revive her. When I got the call, I immediately checked in with the little girl's soul to see what was going on. The soul was quite emphatic that she had been born too soon and wanted to wait and come at a better time, after her brother was born. I asked her how soon all that was going to happen, and she wasn't clear on the exact timing but said that her mother would become pregnant with her brother within that year and then shortly after that, she would be back. Her soul felt bad about putting her parents through such grief; she said she had been in a hurry to get here but should not have jumped ahead of her brother. She also said that her mother would use the wisdom she had gained from this experience to help others. Sure enough, that's what happened. My friend is a local radio personality, and she has since done a lot of work with mothers who have lost a child. An old psychic friend of mine used to say, "Turn your scars into stars" — and that's exactly what she did.

A year later my friend gave birth to a little boy, and two years after that she gave birth to twins, a boy and a girl. She says that her second daughter's personality is just like that of her first daughter, who died.

For those of you who have lost a child, I can guarantee you that your child's soul was gently taken back home and is receiving as much loving care as possible. There are countless wonderful caregivers and angels on the other side who love nurturing whoever needs it. If anyone tells you that the death of your child occurred because God wanted him or her home with Him, please remember that that is a stupid thing that people say when they don't know what else to say. God would never rip your child out of your arms so that He could selfishly have him or her to Himself. No. Death happens to all of us, and we should turn to God — rather than blame Him — to help us heal our grief.

CHAPTER ELEVEN

The White Light, the Tunnel, and Heaven

*E*nough books have been written about near-death experiences to fill a bookstore. Most people who have had such an experience describe a white light as the entrance to heaven. Yet skeptics continue to devise alternative, heaven-free explanations for this nearly universal experience.

I can assure you there truly is a tunnel, a white light, and a place we call heaven. Lilli the angel says we should think of the white light as the porch light at the front door of heaven. I think that's pretty cool! Every deceased person I've ever worked with sees the light — including the earthbound souls who choose not to follow it. The tunnel reminds me of the old days at the airport, when our loved ones would be standing by the gate waiting for us when we arrived. They usually had flowers or balloons to welcome us home, and that's the same kind of scene you'll see in the tunnel — lots of family and friends waiting to welcome their newly deceased loved ones back home.

The day that John F. Kennedy Jr.'s airplane went down, it

was unclear at first if he, his wife, Carolyn, and their friend had died, so I checked in with his soul to see what was happening. I saw him walking into the tunnel and being greeted by his mother and father, which was a wonderful sight to behold. I checked on Carolyn, and she had stayed behind to try to communicate to her mother that she had died but was okay. By the end of the day, I saw her go into the tunnel and head home to John.

In 2011, the book *90 Minutes in Heaven* was a *New York Times* bestseller. Written by Don Piper, an ordained minister, it caught my eye at the grocery store, so I bought it and read it in one evening. It was an interesting read, but I found it disturbing, in that the author doesn't say that the place he went to was one of the many communities that I'm familiar with in heaven. Instead, the book gives the impression that the place he went to represents *all* of heaven.

In the community where he went, everyone believed that you had to accept Jesus Christ as your personal savior in order to get to heaven. When he said that people spent their days singing praises to the Lord, my whole body cringed. Some religions really do believe that God is the kind of egomaniac who demands we spend our days singing his praises nonstop. All I can say to that is, "Are you kidding?!"

My Experience in Heaven

Here is an excerpt from the chapter I wrote on heaven in my book *Echoes of the Soul* (pages 45–55). It recounts an awesome experience I had and may answer many of your questions.

It was the beginning of spring in 1992. The sun was shining, birds were singing, and earth was coming alive again after a long winter in Minnesota. It was Palm Sunday and I was torn between going to church and doing what I wanted to do, which was preparing my garden for planting. I felt like I should be in church, but also that I needed to be in the quiet of my heart and talk to God there. I decided to pass on church and spend that very special time outside.

My brother Michael and I had been on a ghostbusting job the previous night and I went to bed thinking about the other side of the veil. When I woke up that Sunday morning, it was still on my mind. As I was working in my garden, I was thinking of the knowledge about heaven I had gained over the years. I had learned quite a bit from readings I had channeled and had gathered bits and pieces while communicating with the deceased, but I had no real, experiential knowledge. I had been ghostbusting for twenty years and had believed I was sending those souls to a good place, but for some reason that day, I wanted more concrete information.

As I worked in the garden, I asked God if I could please have more knowledge about the other side. I told Him that with all the work I did about death and life after death, I would like to give more information to people about heaven and where they go when they die. I told God that I wouldn't ask Him about it more than this one time, but that I was very open to receiving any knowledge. I was curious as to how He might give me this information, but decided to let it go and see what might happen.

Three days later, after completely forgetting my Palm Sunday prayer, I had the most memorable experience of my career. It was a Wednesday; I had just finished a healing session with Neil, a good friend, and he was heading upstairs from my basement office. My office started to fill with a hazy white energy. I felt strange — weak, as if I was going to collapse. My body seemed like it had fallen asleep, yet I was awake. I was beginning to have an out-of-body experience, but I didn't recognize it right away.

I became aware of a woman, in spirit form, standing in front of me. I couldn't see her face, just the back of her head and her long blonde hair. She said to me, "Let's go, let's go." I felt afraid and asked Neil, who was still on the stairs, if he would help me. I told him something very strange was happening and that a presence was urging me to follow her.

My perception was completely off. I knew on one level that I was in my office but I also felt as if I were in another dimension. Neil shook my body, hoping to stop whatever it was that was happening. It did stop for about fifteen seconds and then it started again — the blonde spirit prompting me to go with her. The feeling I had was familiar — I told Neil it felt as if I were dying. The room continued to fill with white fog and my body became so weak that I wanted to just lie down and let go.

Then I became aware of a tunnel directly in front of me. It was the same tunnel I had seen in so many of my ghostbusting jobs — the one I send the ghosts through and into the light, the tunnel that connects our side to the other side.

One of my guides told me to have Neil call my brother Michael and ask him to come over as quickly as possible, then to get me upstairs and into the living room. Neil called Michael and then dragged me upstairs. By this point, I could barely speak and my legs appeared lifeless. Neil kept telling me to get back into my body and the blonde spirit kept telling me to go with her. He dragged me upstairs to the couch and my body fell into a heap. I felt as if I had no control over what was happening.

Minutes seemed like hours as we waited for my brother to arrive. When Michael finally came, he was fully aware of what was happening. He had talked with his guides on the drive over, and they told him that three days earlier I had asked God to go to the other side. They told him I was being allowed to go and would consciously remember the experience.

He said, "Echo, I am supposed to hold your hand and ground your body while your soul goes to the other side and gathers information." As he was talking I finally realized that I was having an out-of-body experience and that the blonde spirit was my soul trying to get me to let go and take a journey to the other side. I had not told anyone, including my brother, about my prayer on Sunday, so I was amazed at what he said and what was happening.

The Other Side

Michael took my hand and told me that everything was fine, that I should go and that he would be here to protect my body. With his reassurance, I fully left my body, and my conscious mind merged with the blonde spirit that was my soul. I started to float through the tunnel. A loving warmth surrounded me as I moved more fully into it. All throughout the tunnel I could hear a faint voice echoing, "Let go, let go."

Many souls were in the tunnel waiting to greet departing (dying) loved ones. Reunions were taking place around me. Then I saw a bright light ahead, at the end of the tunnel. I floated up, going higher and higher. As I came up to the white light, I remember thinking that I should close my eyes or I would be blinded from its brightness — but I opened my eyes instead and flowed right through it.

I came out on the other side feeling calm and aware. I could see a quaint little village with cobblestone streets. My grandmother was standing there with a friend. She introduced me, and her friend said, "Oh, you didn't tell me she was dying today." My grandmother said, "Oh no, she's not dying, just visiting." I looked closely at my grandma's face. She looked so beautiful — no wrinkles, no stress, just joy. A youthfulness and serenity engulfed her. I looked around and saw several old friends who had died. They didn't come over to me. They just smiled as if they knew I was not to waste any time. They all had that same youthful, serene look on their faces.

Out of nowhere an angel appeared. She was quite lovely, with light, wavy, reddish hair down to her shoulders, a long flowing gown, and, yes, wings. She told me she would be my guide and wanted to show me as much as possible in the limited time we had.

The first place she took me to was called the Pink Place. The entire community had a pink aura around it. It was beautiful. In front of us was a hospital, and even though we were standing some distance from it, I could see inside. It wasn't like a hospital on earth with a lot of medical equipment and personnel. It was more like a resting place, with caregivers. They were not necessarily doctors or nurses but loving souls trying to bring comfort.

Some souls in the hospital were going through an adjustment period, learning to live without their physical bodies. Many had been heavily medicated during their death process and their souls were affected by the drugs. They were resting, healing, and adjusting. Some souls had difficulty accepting their deaths, and caregivers were working with them to help them accept their transition. Some souls from physically handicapped bodies needed help adjusting to life without a challenged body. The whole second floor of the hospital was for suicide victims. Some were asleep, others were dealing with the frustration of taking their lives. Many were still knocked out from the amount of drugs and alcohol they took to cause their deaths.

There were many floors to the hospital, but I didn't have time to investigate. I needed to move on. I saw many souls lying on the grass outside the hospital with their eyes closed. The angel said the Pink Place was for healing and that those souls were healing from the energy that surrounded the community.

Then we floated down a road. First I saw a landscape with rolling hills, lush foliage, grass, flowers, streams, lakes, and rivers. The colors of the flowers were crisp and vivid and the flowers all smelled fragrant. We continued floating over a hill and into a valley, where I saw a huge white and gold coliseum with enormous pillars, windows, and doors, but no glass. I saw angels coming in and out. The angel told me that this is where the angels live who help people on earth.

About this time, I could faintly hear my brother's voice. He was telling me "to go find the music." It was only then that I became aware that there was music playing all around me. I looked at the angel and she motioned me to follow her. We floated to a meadow of singers and musicians. I saw Nat King Cole and then many others that I recognized from this side. Some were writing songs, some were singing. This is a little hard to describe, but there were several kinds of music being played at the same time. It was like a giant radio station and all you had to do was "tune into the vibration" you wanted to hear.

The next city we floated to was particularly important to me. Ever since I was a little girl, Jesus has always been a central figure in my life. Perhaps that's why the angel took me where she did. Or perhaps it was because Easter week was being celebrated on earth. In any case, we were now in a magnificent place, truly a place of beauty. It was very picturesque — blue sky, lush green nature everywhere. Thousands of souls were milling around, very excited about something. It felt as if a celebration were going on; people were very emotional, some cheering, others crying. Still others stood off by themselves, completely captivated by the man in the middle of the crowd. He was speaking or teaching about something. I looked at the angel as if to ask her who the man was and she said it was Jesus. I wondered if it was okay for me to be there. The angel, reading my thoughts, told me it was fine. I was welcome. She had wanted me to experience the City of Jesus, as she called it, knowing what He meant to me.

I felt great joy and awe as I watched Him preach. Here was the man I cherished so much. He was surrounded by a golden aura that radiated wisdom and knowledge. His features were striking — dark shoulder-length hair, a beard, a tanned complexion, and the most intense eyes I had ever seen. Yet the thing I found myself most mesmerized by were His hands; strong, weathered, thousands of years old, full of wisdom and knowledge about all the pain He had healed.

He talked to an enormous crowd of souls about loving one another. His whole message, His whole essence was love. There was such a gentleness about Him. He felt so powerful, and yet He was humble. I wanted to get as close to Him as possible. I remember feeling as if I were truly home, and I didn't want to leave this magnificent city. Everywhere I looked the air seemed charged with hope, with answers.

I could hear my name being called — "Echo, Echo" — over and over. My brother was urging me to return to my body because this experience was very hard on it but I didn't want to leave. Then Michael told me to look for God, and it was then I realized that I was surrounded by God. God was and is everywhere. Just think the word *God* and He/She is there. A presence, or know-ingness. It's hard to describe. It's like standing in a closet and someone says go find the closet and you realize you're in the middle of the closet, but you don't know how to describe it. You are enveloped in it; it's everything around you. You breathe it in. It's part of your thoughts and feelings. You are part of the closet, but at any time you can walk out of the closet and feel separate again. It's hard to describe in words.

I asked the angel what else she could teach me before I returned to my body. She told me that heaven was full of commu-nities and that each reflected a different reality. The reality we live by on earth, the consciousness we hold, determines where we go in heaven. For example, if during your lifetime you were a hard-working German and devout Catholic, when you go to heaven you will live in a community that embraces the same beliefs you have. She showed me a community of beggars and thieves. She said that this is their reality. All day long they steal or beg from one another. Eventually they will grow tired of that way of life and start asking others outside of their community if there is a better way to live. All souls continually move on to different realities, always searching for a better way. People need to evolve in their beliefs in heaven just as they must on earth. Each soul needs to learn and grow toward understanding its oneness with God.

The angel told me that in heaven each community has a class-room and an instructor who teaches the reality of that group. As souls advance, there is no longer a need for some communities and they will no longer exist.

I said that it seemed so complicated to have so many communities with varying realities. She said that it is actually less complicated than it is on earth, for in heaven everyone is clear about each other's reality. If you live in a community different from others', you have a different belief system than they do. It's that simple. She said that it's more complex on earth because we believe that we all have the same reality when, in fact, we don't. She said that's why we have so many problems on earth, because we have trouble honoring each other's convictions. We don't want to accept that everyone has a different reality; we want everyone to be and think and act like us.

I asked the angel about movie stars because I am such a movie buff and she said that they also have their community and may live there if they choose to remain that star. Some who cross over desire a change from their movie star identity and go to a community that better reflects their individuality and reality. I saw John F. Kennedy's soul while I was doing a reading for someone. I asked him how long he was going to remain JFK, and he told me that as long as there was a need for people to meet him, he would remain on the other side rather than reincarnate. He told me that he was one of the first people, after relatives, that people ask to meet. He showed me an image of himself shaking many hands, greeting people, and enjoying what he was doing.

Once again I heard my brother sternly calling me back. My body was having a difficult time. My breathing was very labored and Michael could feel my energy level was extremely low. I could tell by the tone of his voice that I had to go, and I quickly flowed back to the light. To my right I saw a broad stairway and I asked the angel where it led. She said that there are several levels to heaven. The highest level is where we all have the same reality, where we know we are one with God and we live in peace with one another.

I asked the angel one last question. Was the village with the cobblestone streets, where I had arrived, the entrance point into heaven? She said it was one of many places throughout heaven where people arrive. Some went directly to the hospital, others went to entry points determined by their consciousness. She said that she wished she could teach me and show me so much more, but my body was really suffering and I had to go back. As soon as she spoke those words, my soul jolted back into my body.

When I took this conscious journey out of the body, I used all the energy in my soul to do it. My body experienced a great deal of difficulty while I was out. I was like a rag doll, lifeless and limp. After my soul came back in, it took at least twenty minutes before I could speak. My tongue was thick, my eyes were hard to open and very sensitive to light. It was a great effort to move my body for some time. At least an hour passed before I felt normal again. As soon as I was able to go to bed, I slept for twelve hours.

Now you should have a sense of what it's like on the other side. If you want to know more, *Echoes of the Soul* includes another ten pages of information about heaven, and the rest of this chapter also has more details.

In Between Lifetimes

The Elders recommend that each soul spend a minimum of sixty years on the other side before reincarnating into a new life so that it can heal issues from its previous incarnation. The process of healing old issues to prevent bringing them into the new life can take quite a while, depending on the person's desire and willingness to heal. Some souls choose to reincarnate much more quickly, before they have finished healing, which means they bring all their former issues in with them to their new life. Also, souls who come back too quickly after their previous incarnation tend to have quite a bit of confusion about who they are, what life this is, and what family they're in. Sixty years on the other side might sound like a long time, but it feels like only a moment to the souls there, as they have no clocks, calendars, or awareness of time.

When it's time to be reborn into a new life, either souls have a gut knowing that they're ready or the Elders advise them that it's time to begin preparing. About a year's worth of planning goes into writing up the blueprint for the new life and then choosing the family that will best help the souls accomplish their goals.

Hell and Middle Heaven

Some of you may be wondering about hell. Lilli told me that there is a community in heaven that resembles a hell, but it was not created by God; she said God would never create or send anyone to such a place. It was created by our consciousness. We have created it from our religious beliefs of what hell is supposed to be like, and because some people go through life believing they are going to hell, they perpetuate the existence of this place in heaven. Lilli told me that at some point, when we've all raised our consciousness enough, there will be no such place. If you do go to this hell community when you die, it's because you believe that it is where you are supposed to go.

In the past ten years, while during readings, I have become familiar with a place that I call middle heaven simply because it looks like it's located right in the middle of heaven. It reminds me of a gated community or retirement village, and in this sense "retirement" has to do with being retired from earth — retired from checking in on family members, obsessing about what's happening down here, feeling responsible for visiting living loved ones. Retired.

The one factor common in this community is that all residents have been dead for a minimum of twenty years. If you're a psychic medium trying to locate someone and you can't find them, ask the person who's seeking communication how long they've been gone. If it's twenty years or longer, they may have emotionally detached themselves from life here on earth and may be residing in middle heaven, which means they may not answer your call.

❄

One of the reasons I've written this book is to emphasize the importance of our spiritual development and our relationship with God while we're here. If we know our oneness with God in this life, we automatically know it when we go home. As a wise departed woman told me, "When everything is said and done, the only thing that matters is God."

CHAPTER TWELVE

After-Death Communication

*I*n the 1989 movie *Always*, Richard Dreyfus plays a fire-fighting pilot who dies when his plane goes down. In the next scene, he is sitting on a tree stump while an angel, played by Audrey Hepburn, is explaining to him that he's now going to be a guide for a younger fire pilot. He asks her how the man will hear him since he's dead, and she tells him to just *think* to him and he will get the thoughts. She goes on to say, "That's how we communicate with them now, through thoughts. They think it's their own thoughts, but it doesn't matter. At least they get the message." Those may not be the exact words because it's been years since I saw the movie, but it's pretty close and you get my drift. That's how our spirit guides, our deceased loved ones, and God communicate to us — and that's how we will communicate to our living loved ones when we pass away.

Learning to Communicate through Thoughts

Communicating through thoughts is called mental telepathy, and it's part of the psychic gift called clairaudience. We frequently communicate this way in our everyday life, but a lot of us don't pay much attention to it. For example, can you remember a time when someone's name came into your head and a few seconds later they called or texted or you ran into them? When this happens, we tend to dismiss it as just a coincidence, but in reality we are communicating with the person telepathically. Unfortunately, when we suddenly have a thought of someone we know, instead of stopping to listen to what other thoughts about that person are coming in, usually we simply move on to the next thought — one of the thousand other thoughts we have in a day — and don't think much of it.

When we think about another person suddenly, either the thought comes in from that person or we initiate the thought, and it's easy to differentiate between the two. Here's what I mean. If a song comes on the radio that reminds you of someone, or you see a person who looks like someone you know, or there is some other external trigger, and you start thinking of them, chances are, no matter where they are in the world, they will get a thought of you; in that case, you have initiated the thought. On the other hand, if a thought of someone comes into your mind seemingly out of nowhere, without a trigger, then they initiated it; they had the original thought of you and you picked up on it.

I tell my students in my psychic development classes to follow up on the thoughts that come in from people throughout the day to see if those people were thinking of them. If you think of a friend or loved one on your lunch break, call them that evening and ask if they were thinking of you. It's fun when you realize how strong your thoughts can be.

This brings up a very important point about after-death communication. When you die, your loved ones here will be very sad, and you will probably visit them a lot in the beginning to try to reassure them that you are okay and that you really did live on. The problem is that they will be waiting to hear your voice again, but they won't hear it, because you'll be communicating with them telepathically. If they're not accustomed to this kind of communication, most likely they won't consciously notice your attempts at communication and will think you've forgotten them. As silly as this might sound, if you start practicing sending thoughts now, while you're alive, you'll be able to communicate more effectively when you're deceased. Practice with people who you will probably want to communicate with after death. You don't have to tell them the exact reason why you want to learn how to be a good sender and receiver, unless they've got an understanding of all this.

At their live events, the psychic mediums John Edward and James Van Praagh choose volunteers out of the crowd and give them readings. When asked how they choose who they read, they always say that the loudest soul coming through gets their attention. What that means is that that soul has learned to make its thoughts very strong and loud in order to be heard by the mediums here on earth. How do we make our thoughts loud and strong? By practicing.

When my dad lived in San Francisco and I lived here in Minneapolis, every Thursday we would practice mental telepathy. We had set times throughout the day — 10, 2, 6, and 10 — when we would send thoughts to each other and focus on what thoughts were coming in. We would write down whatever came into our minds, and then we would compare notes the next day. It was really fun and helped both of us become stronger at sending and receiving.

Contacting Deceased Loved Ones

If you want to communicate with a deceased loved one, you should say their name out loud to get their attention. They do not sit in heaven listening to our every thought and waiting around for us to think of them. There will be times when they don't answer because they have lives going on over there, contrary to many of our conceptions.

When we covered this subject recently in my advanced psychic class, I gave the students my dad's name to use for practice communicating with the deceased. Many of them said that Dad was irritated because so many of them were calling him to talk to them. Dad was an outgoing guy, so it didn't occur to me that this exercise would irritate him, but it makes sense that he's got things going on over there and wouldn't enjoy being pulled on by twenty students wanting to communicate with him!

I recently discovered something very cool that had never occurred to me. Being in the line of work that I'm in, I've seen many living people pull on their deceased loved ones by asking them to come and visit, to make decisions for them, or to come and comfort them. I know how hard that is on the deceased, so I was delighted when my angel Lilli told me that we can leave messages for our loved ones. As soon as she said so, I saw an image of someone on the other side taking messages for people from their living loved ones. I also saw the deceased picking up their messages throughout the day. To leave a message for someone, all you need to do is say your name, the other person's name, and the message you want to leave, like this: "This is Echo Bodine. Please leave a message for my mom, Mae, and tell her I love her." You won't necessarily hear back from them, but they will know you were thinking of them, and that will put a smile on their face. If they do choose to respond, you'll hear a simple thought in your head, such as "I love you too," or "Thank you."

If you try to contact your loved one and feel like you're not getting any response, I want you to understand that it's not that easy for the deceased to communicate to us. It's easier for them to communicate with psychics trained in mediumship because the psychics have learned how to raise their energy to almost the same level as that of the deceased.

Also, in the first few months after their passing, you need to be mindful that the deceased are getting used to the "new neighborhood." It might not be feasible for them to come back to the old neighborhood just because you want them to. If you are not able to connect with them yourself (which, as I said, is not that easy, so don't get discouraged) you can go to the Referrals section of my website, www.echobodine.com/referrals, to find a reputable, trustworthy medium.

This reminds me of a comment late-night comedian Craig Ferguson made when his father passed away. He said during his monologue that many psychics had contacted him saying that they could communicate to his father for him, and Craig said, "That would be amazing because I was never able to communicate with him when he was living."

Is a Deceased Loved One Trying to Contact You?

Without a medium, the easiest way for the deceased to talk to us is through what seem like dreams but are in fact actual soul visitations. Bits and pieces of these dream encounters come through to the conscious mind. If you wake up in the morning feeling like a dream was *real* and the dream stays with you for hours, this is a sign that you have been visited.

Another easy way for souls to get our attention is through smell. They can actually think a smell, and we pick it up as a smell thought. Have you ever had an experience when, say, a smell of your grandma's perfume seemed to permeate the room for just a second or two and it instantly made you think of her? She did that. Or maybe a loved one was a heavy smoker and you smelled the smoke. A Brazilian healer friend of mine named Alberto Aguas died in 1992. He wore this amazing cologne from France that I've never smelled here in the U.S., but when he comes to visit he projects that smell and there's no mistaking that it's him visiting. I love it when that happens!

Also, if your deceased loved one is able to manipulate energy (there are good teachers on the other side who teach souls how to do this), they may move material things to get your attention.

If you think a loved one is trying to contact you, make sure to ask for good, solid proof that it's really them. There are ill-intentioned earthbound souls out there who love to mess with grieving people, so ask for specific memories the two of you shared that prove they are who they say they are (and be prepared to send this kind of proof after you die when you contact your loved ones from the other side).

People Are in Death as They Were in Life

Many people think that when a person dies, they become angelic and lose their character defects. Unfortunately, that's not true, as you'll quickly discover when you communicate with your deceased loves ones. Yes, some of our perspectives do change when we're out of these earthly bodies, but, as is the case when we are on earth, if we don't want to change our perspectives, we don't have to.

I had an interesting learning experience during a medium reading I did for a woman and her mother-in-law, who came to communicate with the husband/son who had been deceased for a couple of years. Usually when there is a reunion in a reading, everyone is pretty happy to see one another and it's a pleasant experience for all who are present at the party. In this particular case, this young man taught me they aren't always pleasant. I called his name, and into my office came this guy who wanted to know "what the hell these two want." He went on to say, "They bugged me when I was living, and now they're bugging me when I'm dead." I was a bit flabbergasted, to say the least.

I wasn't sure what to say to the women. I didn't want to hurt their feelings, so I sat there waiting for him to say something nice. Finally the wife stepped in and asked me if he was being "crabby." I sheepishly answered, "Kinda." She asked if he was bugged that they were there asking about him, and he sent a resounding *yes* into my head. I told her he didn't seem very happy, and both the mother and the wife were thrilled with this information. They confirmed that, yes, this was her husband, her son, and that he had always been cranky in life and it made sense to them that he would be this way in death. They told me that if I had said he was really sweet and so glad to see both of them, they would have thought I was a fraud, but the fact that I described his unhappy personality to them was all the proof they needed that his soul was alive and doing fine on the other side. The wife said she was hoping he had mellowed a bit since his death, but they were content just hearing from him. The mother was relieved that he wasn't in hell.

Another common misconception is that once we're dead we

"see the light" (so to speak) and feel bad about the unkind things we did or said to people. Many women have asked me if their deceased husbands will see how mean they were to them when the husbands were alive. I wish I could say that everything will become crystal clear for everyone when they get over to the other side, but it just doesn't work that way. It can take quite a while on the other side before some souls want to take a good hard look at their behavior toward others. We all have to eventually, but it doesn't necessarily happen right away. Denial is just as rampant in heaven as it is on earth.

I remember the week that O. J. Simpson's wife was murdered and everyone was speculating about who did it. I was teaching a psychic development class, and my students asked me if I would tune in to Nicole Brown Simpson's soul and ask her who killed her. I was quite surprised to see her on the other side telling a large group of people that Kato Kaelin, the pool guy, was the one who killed her, and she was in shock over it. I asked the guide who worked with me at the time what he thought about what she said, and he said that souls can choose to see whatever they want, no matter what side of the veil they are on. He said that death does not automatically make people privy to the secrets of the universe or of their own life, that she would eventually get to a place in her growth where she would be willing to see the truth, and that maybe she was already there.

The spirits have never said that O.J. did or did not "do it." My point is that dying does not guarantee that we will be ready to see the truth afterward. But regardless of whether we can recognize or acknowledge truths when we get to the other side, everything that happens is a karmic experience for all involved and everyone gets their just (as in, *justice*) karma eventually.

Another misconception we have about the deceased is that

once they are on the other side, they no longer care about what goes on down here and they're just happy, happy, happy. That's not true. It's like graduating from high school or college, when we feel a bittersweet happiness that our long journey of education has ended. This is very similar to how the soul feels about the life here that is over.

In medium readings, I've also noticed that living people often try to get their deceased loved ones to advise them because they think souls on the other side are all-knowing, but they're not. They have psychic abilities only if they cultivated those abilities while they were alive. Plus, the deceased intuitively know that they're not supposed to interfere with people's lives, so they are generally not forthcoming when loved ones ask them about the future.

I have two more stories of after-death communication to share, both of which illustrate that people are still themselves on the other side and that they still feel very human emotions.

QUESTIONS AND APOLOGIES FROM A DECEASED TWIN

Five years ago, my friend Marta lost her twin brother, Mark, at age forty. They were both TV producers, and Mark had finished a big project that day. He and his business partner celebrated with a beer, and then Mark said he needed to lie down for a while because he was feeling a bit woozy. About an hour later his partner checked on him and found him dead from what the coroner later said were natural causes. Marta called me at 2:30 AM to give me the news, and I immediately checked in on Mark's soul. For some reason, maybe because he was young, I expected to find him wide awake and ready to communicate, but instead his soul was sound asleep. I asked my spirit helpers if they could shed any light on what had happened, and this is what I learned:

An Elder from the other side came down even before Mark lay down, and waited for him to go to sleep. Today was the day he was to graduate, and as soon as he fell asleep, the Elder lifted his soul out of his body and took him to the other side, where he continued to sleep. His body died shortly afterward. His parents, who were both on the other side, were nearby, waiting to see him, and his mother was impatient. She was pacing back and forth and kept saying that she just wanted to check on him and make sure he was okay. The Elders kept reassuring her that he was fine and needed to wake up on his own, and she wasn't very happy with that answer.

Then they told me that when Mark and Marta and the Elders were in the planning stages of their current lives, Mark felt that he would have accomplished everything he wanted by age forty, and then he would help Marta with her work from the other side.

They also said that early the following Tuesday morning, Mark's soul would wake up and there would be a meeting between him, his parents, four Elders, and some of his deceased friends and relatives to help him remember his life plan and what was going on. The meeting would be over by noon, and sometime in the afternoon Marta would start to feel his energy.

In addition, they said that Mark would do many things in the coming weeks and months to let his twin know he was around her and that once he got into the groove of his new life on the other side he was going to do very well. They suggested that Marta make a scrapbook of Mark's life.

The following Tuesday, after the meeting was to have taken place, I checked in with his soul to see if he was awake, and he was. He related a lot of information to me, most of which he wanted me to convey to Marta.

He told me that he needed Marta to explain to him the life plan and especially the part about his leaving at an early age because he couldn't remember it and he trusted her. He was having a hard time because he felt like he had abandoned Marta and kept apologizing over and over.

He kept saying that he didn't get it — it didn't make sense to him that he was physically dead. Then I heard him repeating the name David over and over in his head, and he seemed very concerned about this David.

He told me he had spent time with his parents. He said he felt very close to his dad and saw a wisdom in him that was even stronger than it was when he was living. He said that his mom had changed and was not as selfish and freaked out as she had been in life, that she'd become more loving, gentler. He said his dad was being really patient with her.

Again he mentioned David and said he needed reassurance from Marta that everyone wouldn't forget him. He showed me a box of cereal and said he wished he had eaten more cereal. He said he found himself thinking about stupid things like that rather than what would be considered the all-important things.

He wished he had played with Marta's two young daughters more than he had. He also said he was glad that Marta had her husband, Nelson, and that Nelson was a good man.

He said that it had been hard to give Marta signs. He saw her looking at his body when she went to identify him, and said he was glad she did. (She hadn't wanted to look, but her best friend talked her into it.) Quickly he said, "Grandma says hi," and explained that she had been really nice to him since he got to heaven. He ended it by saying, "You haven't heard the last of me. Thank you for helping me through this — this has been hard." With that he faded out. For someone who had been deceased for only a few days, Mark mustered quite a bit of energy to say all that.

I asked Marta if she knew who David was, and she said that was the name Mark had wanted and that his father had wanted to call him David as well. Instead, because they were twins, Mark's mother had thought the pair should have similar names. This could have been Mark's way of letting Marta know this was really him we were communicating with.

I share this story with you for a number of reasons. This was a great example of the deceased needing our help when it comes to accepting their death. Deceased people don't automatically remember their life plan when they die. It takes time for them to remember, especially in a case like Mark's, where he lay down for a nap and woke up in heaven four days later. That would be shocking for anyone.

It's also notable that he kept apologizing for abandoning Marta. I've heard this from many people on the other side. They feel full of remorse for leaving their loved ones behind, and if they've left a lot of unfinished business for the living to tend to, they feel even worse.

REGRETS ON BOTH SIDES

Jim, an ex-boyfriend of mine, called with terrible news. Donna, his beloved wife of five years, was dead. I tell you this story to emphasize our need to take care of business while we are alive.

Jim told me that he left for work in the morning, "kissing her good-bye and telling her I loved her." Donna said, "I love you too," and drifted back to sleep.

But at about 10:30 that morning, Donna's boss called Jim to say that Donna had not yet come in. Because she'd recently had lots of health problems — including a stroke on their wedding day — he was concerned. Still, despite her health challenges, she was young and had always rallied.

Jim clocked out of work and ran home to see if Donna had overslept, but when he walked into the bedroom, he knew right away that his fifty-one-year-old wife was dead.

The whole time Jim was telling me this story, I could see Donna standing between here and the other side, just listening to him. She was listening to the way he spoke about her, listening to him talk about her children and the poor health she had suffered for so many years. Tears were streaming down her face as she watched him trying to cope with the experience all alone. She wanted so badly to reach out to him and tell him that everything was going to be okay, but she had to stand back and let him have this experience. She loved hearing him talk about some of their memories. At one point in the conversation, she needed to leave for a while because it all became too emotional for her. She didn't want to be dead. She wanted to be alive and healthy. She wanted to be with her husband and her children!

When Jim asked me, "Why now? Why did she have to die now, when she was getting better?" I heard her say that when she had almost died the previous August from complications from a stroke, she had asked the powers that be if she could have one more Christmas with him, since that was their favorite holiday. So she was given the extra time.

The next morning when I woke up, she was standing next to my bed with a very concerned look on her face. I was a bit startled. We had never met in person, but I knew from the previous day who she was. She told me she was concerned about her son because her husband didn't like him, and she was worried that Jim would treat him unfairly at the funeral. She asked me if there was anything I could do. I wasn't sure, but I gave Jim a call to see how he was doing. He immediately started talking about her son and said that he didn't want him at the funeral, and the only thing I could think to say was, "What would your wife want?" I kept bringing the conversation back to that every time he brought up the son. Donna did attend her funeral and was glad to see her son there, and everything turned out fine with the family.

About a week later I got another call from Jim. He was upset because Donna's estate was such a mess. She had never had a will drawn up and had a different password for all her important accounts — none of which he could find. He was beside himself with grief and frustration. When I got off the phone, I asked Donna why, with all the health problems she'd had, she hadn't gotten her affairs in order. She told me that she had felt intuitive nudges to get things in order but was afraid that if she did so she *would* die. I hear this from many people, and it's understandable. But you need to know that the end result with Jim and Donna was one grieving partner on this side dealing with a lot of frustration, and Donna on the other side feeling regret.

On this side or the other, life does go on for all of us. We need to take care of our nuts-and-bolts, nitty-gritty business for others, just as we hope they will take care of their business for us. The Golden Rule applies on both sides of the veil!

CHAPTER THIRTEEN

My Mom's Dying Process

*E*arlier in the book you read about my dear, sweet mama. She finally made her transition on October 4, 2012. The process she went through during the last six months of her life was very special to me. We had many out-of-body experiences together, including trips to the other side to get things in order for her new life.

This may sound strange, but I don't think our experience was exceptional. Yes, Mom and I were both tuned in to our psychic abilities, but you may have had similar experiences. I want to share the story of her dying to help you recognize if you have been through similar experiences and to help you recognize such experiences if you go through them in the future. If you have lost a loved one recently, think back to the six months leading up to their passing and recall if there was anything different in their behavior. Did they sleep more? Did they seem spacey, as if their "mind was elsewhere"? Did they make remarks to you about death or do things to get their affairs in order?

For example, my mom had a grocery delivery service that brought her groceries every two weeks. Two weeks before she passed, she told them she would no longer be needing their service. On my birthday in September, she told me that she would not make it to my brother's birthday, which was at the end of October. Each day that she was alive felt as if she were closing up shop. Our phone conversations always had a sense of finality, and I never knew when I hung up if that would be the last time I would talk to her.

About three years before Mom died, I had many dreams of the two of us going to the other side. There was a man over there she was particularly fond of, and she wanted me to know someone special was waiting for her.

The first few times we went over, he always had his back to me, and his energy was not very pleasant. He seemed quite self-centered, as though he thought everything was about him. I always felt as though he was keeping his face from me so that I couldn't see the real him. Whenever I woke up from those dreams, I felt frustrated that she was attracted to the same type of guy on the other side as she had always been drawn to on this side!

A little time passed, and in one of the dreams Mom told me she had resolved her stuff with Self-Centered Guy and wanted me to meet a new man. I remember feeling ambivalent about meeting him because I didn't want to find out that he was just like the other guy. In at least half a dozen dreams, we went over to meet him, but I always resisted it and the dream would end without our meeting.

About eight months before Mom passed, my resistance shifted and I finally met him. This man was much gentler with Mom and very caring. She was like a schoolgirl around him, and it was fun to watch them interact. I felt a sense of peace, knowing that there was someone loving waiting for her on the other side.

A note about this kind of astral projection: As I've said, our souls leave our bodies at night and during the day when our body takes downtime, such as when we are daydreaming or taking a quick nap. We are not limited in where we can go, and traveling to the other side is not unusual. Out-of-body dreams feel like an *experience*, rather than just a dream, and much of what happens on the other side ends up a blur when we wake up because if we remembered all that we saw and did over there, we would likely wake up feeling sad that we didn't get to stay. We often have a lingering feeling throughout the day of being "homesick."

During the last six weeks of Mom's life, she was napping all the time, and my dreams of visiting the other side with her were becoming more and more of a blur. I knew a shift was happening, and I could feel that her soul was very busy. Then about one week before her death, all the dreams stopped and it felt like everything was in place for her to make her transition.

The morning she died didn't feel any different from any other day. I'd always wondered if I would have a knowing of when she was going to pass, but nothing stood out on that day.

The day before, October 3, had some warning signs that the end was near, but it wasn't like some strong psychic message from on high. I woke up that day with a very heavy feeling on my chest, almost like Mom was sitting there trying to get my attention. I called her right away to see if something was wrong, and she said she was very upset because she'd had a dream that someone was trying to turn her into a worm. Her blood pressure was very high, and the assisted-living aides were concerned. She said she was very tired and just wanted to sleep, and she asked me to tell my siblings not to call her that day because she needed sleep. When we hung up I felt a heaviness in the air and wanted to call her back and have her reassure me that she was okay, but intuitively I had the sense to leave her alone.

Throughout the day I tuned in to her psychically to see how she was doing. She felt far, far away, so I let her be. I usually called her at night to see how she was before she went to bed, but that night I had the feeling I shouldn't.

The next morning an aide came in to get her up and found her lying on the floor, awake, which was very unusual because she hadn't been able to walk on her own for several weeks. It was as if she had known she was going somewhere and tried getting up to go. The aides got her back on her couch and left her alone for a couple of hours. Another aide, who she had become very close friends with, came in to make her some tea, and Mom told her she was having a rough morning and declined the tea. This was very unusual, as she loved her morning tea. When the aide came back at noon to bring her lunch, she took her last breath and passed away. She had always had a fear of being alone when she died, and I think she was hanging on until someone was there with her.

As much as you think you're prepared for the end of your loved one's life, it's pretty shocking when you actually get the phone call that they have died. I was coming out of the pet store when my brother called to say, "We got the call. Mom just died." I felt like someone had punched my whole nervous system. My body started to shake, and I stopped breathing. I put myself mentally and emotionally on hold so that I could drive home. I couldn't think. I didn't know what to do. I needed someone to guide me through this, and that person would normally have been Mom.

I called the most rational person I knew — my son's father, Roman — and told him that Mom had just passed away and I needed him to tell me what to do. All I could think was that I was now the elder in the family and so should know what to do. But I needed someone to tell me what that was. I kept saying, "Tell me what to do," over and over. His advice was simple and very helpful: he said to cry my eyes out when I was alone and to be strong when I was with my family. He also said, "Grief comes in waves, and the best thing you can do is learn to ride the waves." About fifteen minutes after our conversation, I felt an energy circle around me that I can only describe as God's Grace. I was lifted up out of that awful sadness I was in and stayed in an altered state for over a week.

My family all met at Mom's apartment that day and sat with her body for six hours. She lay on the couch with a blanket covering everything but her face, and we took turns sitting near her, stroking her hair, holding her hand. We reminisced as a family and made funeral arrangements. We cried a lot and laughed at silly memories. Sitting with a deceased body for six hours may sound creepy, but I have to say that that day is one of the most memorable of my life. We united as a family, and it was something beyond words.

Many people have asked me if I felt Mom's soul around us that day and I did, twice. Her energy was incredibly light, almost like a whisper, and my sister felt it as well. Mom guided me to pick out her clothes for the reviewal (also known as a viewing). She didn't have words to talk to us, but we felt her presence ever so slightly.

We had a lot of her things to go through, but we decided to come back another day to begin tackling that job. We needed that first day to be as simple as possible. Our precious mom had died, and we needed to just be with it.

We chose to have an open casket at her reviewal so that people could come and see her one last time. My sister-in-law Katie made amazing picture boards of Mom from the time she was a little girl all the way up to the present, and people loved seeing the photos.

In the months since she passed away, I've learned a great deal about losing someone this dear to me. When our dad passed away, it was a relief for all of us because he had been a tough man to deal with. We were sad but also relieved. Mom was a completely different story. She was our mom and there is no way anyone will ever be able to replace her.

❋

Reviewals, wakes, and funerals are definitely for the living. It was wonderful to see so many people come to Mom's service for us, the grieving family. The cards, flowers, and money were all wonderful gestures of love. One friend gave me a gift certificate to our local grocery store so that I could get food at the deli and not have to think about cooking. My cousin Mary owns a grocery store and had food and water sent over to the chapel for members of our family so that we could take breaks and get our energy replenished. People were absolutely wonderful.

Grief is a very ominous feeling. It's numb, sad, lonely, angry, fearful. Your brain blanks out from time to time. You're restless but you can't sleep, and when you do sleep, you're still restless. It feels shocking and empty, and according to everyone who's been through it, all of this is normal.

People have asked me why I haven't cried much since she passed, and I realize it's because I've been grieving her loss bit by bit for a long while. When she stopped driving, I cried. When she went from walking on her own to using a wheelchair, I cried. When her memory started to fade, I cried. I cried when she no longer had energy to attend holiday gatherings with the family. I cried as she lost interest in bingo, food, and her favorite TV shows. As I watched her go from being a clearheaded, wise woman to having the personality of a little girl, I cried.

When she had tough days, I cried. When she no longer could take care of her beloved bird, Shuggy, I cried. Every time we had another medical emergency, I cried. Every time I saw a part of her die, I cried.

About a week after she passed, I was at the grocery store walking around in a complete daze. I couldn't remember what I had come there for, and I started to cry. I wanted to grab the loudspeaker and announce to the entire store that my sweet mama had just died and I couldn't remember why I was there. At times like this, we often want to tell the whole world that our loved one died so that when we do goofy things like drive away from the gas station with the gas pump nozzle still in the car, or we can't remember our best friend's name, or we buy things we don't need just because we want a distraction, people will just come and hug us instead of making judgments. We want people to know we're coping as best we can, while not coping very well at all.

Visitations from Mom

Because of my psychic abilities, the one question I've heard from just about everyone is, "Have you communicated with your mom since her passing?" I'm happy to say that we've had several communications so far.

Sunday morning, four days after her death, I heard her say, "I want a real cup of coffee." It was so fun to hear her, and I responded by saying out loud, "Okay, Mom, I'll go make us some coffee!" The day before, I was at the grocery store and saw the most beautiful bouquet of pink roses, which were always Mom's favorite. My first reaction was great sadness at not being able to buy them for her, and then my second thought was to buy the roses for her anyway because she would be coming by to visit soon. My sadness disappeared as I put them in a pretty vase for her to enjoy. I set a cup of coffee right next to her roses and told her to come and enjoy them.

Her second visitation took place on a Saturday night. I was sewing a fleece top for a friend, and I suddenly felt this very comforting energy wrap completely around me and heard her as clear as a bell say, "Can you believe this finally happened?" I answered out loud, "I know, Mom. Isn't this strange that you are physically dead?" I felt I was in an altered state, as if the veil to the other side had opened up and we were right there together. It didn't feel far away, as the veil usually feels. Instead it felt like it was just beyond this consciousness, this world. I asked her if she had been back to visit her apartment, and she said, "Ish, no! That's where the hardest part of my life was. That's where I went to die."

My mind was racing with questions I wanted to ask her about what if felt like to live in heaven and what she had been through since dying, but the phone rang and startled me back into this reality. It was my psychic brother, Michael, calling. He could sense something was going on over here but wasn't sure what it was. When I hung up the phone I wanted to get back to the conversation with Mom, but I could no longer feel her.

Remember Mom's male friend, the one waiting for her on the other side? I recently had a heavenly visit with my sweet mama in which she showed me the home that she had been so busy preparing and the man she was living with. Mom looked like she did when she was in her thirties, and she had her energy back. She was very proud of her home and all that she had accomplished in her new life. She told me that our accomplishments on earth build our home in heaven and that all that we've built here continues over there. Her fellow had all white hair and seemed very nice. The energy between them was as if they had known each other forever. It was so, so nice to see Mom like this. The only thing about her that was dead was her physical body. Her soul was very much alive, and she was happy that her journey on earth had ended.

My mother was a gifted spiritual psychic, and I'm looking forward to having many more talks about the other side with her. I'm not sure what's in store, but maybe the next book you'll see from me will be *Conversations with Mom from the Other Side*!

CHAPTER FOURTEEN

Coping with Loss

$\mathcal{T}$he last funeral I attended was for my dear friend Buck, who was killed in a head-on collision with three of his children in the car. A woman swerved over the median and killed my friend and two of his children instantly. His oldest daughter ended up in the hospital with several broken bones. His wife and youngest child had left earlier in the day to attend a family reunion, and he was on his way to join them.

There had to have been at least three hundred people at the standing-room-only funeral, and the energy was so intense with grief I had to leave. Whoever was officiating at that service had to feel an enormous responsibility to bring some kind of comfort to all those people. We say things like "they're in a better place" or "God wanted them home with Him," but does hearing those words really help when we are hurting so bad from the loss of someone we dearly love? Death can seem incredibly senseless no matter how much we try to spin a reason for it.

The Many Faces of Grief

One of my friends gained two hundred pounds when her mom died. Another friend spent a year in bed after losing her child, and another dear friend spent a year in a casino trying to gamble his grief away. When my dad died, I was in the process of painting the outside of my house a nice sage green to go with the color schemes of the other houses in the neighborhood. The day after Dad's funeral, I was thinking about how short life is and that I'd always wanted to live in a yellow house. I stopped painting it green and now live in a pretty yellow house that sticks out like a sore thumb in my neighborhood but always makes me smile.

We all deal with grief in our own way. Many turn to addictions like shopping, gambling, hoarding, alcohol, drugs, eating, and even bingo. Many people I know who had been smoke-free for years started smoking again when they lost a loved one. We try to find ways to dull the pain, but they are all just temporary fixes, if even that. Imagine coming out of the "grief fog" and discovering you've gained two hundred pounds or you've maxed out all your credit cards buying things that are still in their boxes.

Death can definitely shake up our faith. We start thinking about this God guy and wondering why he took our loved ones away from us. We turn to our religion, but the words don't soothe us like they once did. Now we just have more questions. Is there really a heaven? Do we really live after death? Are all these people who write books about life after death just saying these things to sell books and make money? We want death to make sense to us so that it won't hurt so bad.

This is where spirituality comes in. A high percentage of my students come to my psychic and healing classes because they've lost someone dear to them and they are trying to understand life and death in a different way. A high majority of the emails I get start out with the person telling me they got on this path because they lost someone dear to them. People don't just wake up one morning and say, "My life is going so well, I think I'll get on a spiritual path."

Unfortunately, most people make big changes only when pushed hard to do so. Loss is one of the toughest life experiences that pushes us. We have a huge array of amazing people, books, workshops, seminars, and so on available to us to help us heal our grief and get on a spiritual path.

I have written eleven books, and of those eleven, I highly recommend two for people who are suffering from loss: *Echoes of the Soul* and *Look for the Good and You'll Find God*. Then you can move on to *A Still, Small Voice* and *My Big Book of Healing*.

Many clients have come to me for laying-on-of-hands healing when dealing with the loss of someone, and you may want to read up on that. *Hands That Heal* was my very first book, and it covers that subject. Also, I have a program called Healing Pen Pals that is available to you for free. To participate, send an email to www.echobodine.com/healingpenpals and give us your name, the city and state you live in, and what you would like healing for, and our coordinator will assign a healer to you for fifteen days, free of charge. Many people request this kind of healing when they are suffering from a loss.

We have many, many solutions available to us here, as well as on the other side.

Some Tips about Grieving

I want to share some of the really helpful things I've learned in my journey of grief since my mom's death.

- Eat as much protein and as many vegetables as you can and try not to drown your grief in sugar. It's a lot better for your entire body if you cry out your grief rather than stuff it down with a Twinkie (or ten).

- Don't starve yourself, either. Be kind to your body and give it the fuel it needs to get through your grief.

- Don't answer the phone if you're not in the mood to talk. But do pick up the phone and call friends when you need to. Many people feel awkward about knowing what to say to others when they're grieving, and you can let your friends know that they don't have to say the perfect words or fix your pain. You just need someone to listen to you while you talk about your loved one for a while.

- Your temper will have a short fuse during the grieving process, so if you get upset with someone, count to ten or twenty before lashing out at them. You may be overreacting to a situation — grief makes us do that.

- Pace yourself as you go through your loved one's belongings. You may feel inclined to quickly get rid of everything so as not to prolong this part of the process, but slow down and find joy in the memories the things hold. When my brothers, sister, and I started the process of going through Mom's stuff, I dreaded it. But it turned out to be a meaningful and even fun time. We laughed, cried, and reminisced. We didn't pressure ourselves to get it all done in a day. We scheduled one day a week for a month for all of us to go over there together.

- It's proper etiquette to send thank-you notes for

cards and money no later than two weeks after the funeral, but I took my time with it. I did a few cards at a time and wrote heartfelt thanks to these thoughtful people. I waited until my mind was clear enough to know what I was saying.

- I strongly recommend that you have an open casket for viewing the body. Many years ago a mortician friend of mine told me that he sees less grief in people who are able to view their deceased loved one a last time before they are buried or cremated. I was so glad we had an open casket for my mom. The funeral home did an outstanding job of making her look pretty and peaceful, and we all needed that extra time with her before finally saying good-bye. My generation grew up with open caskets during funerals, so it was no big deal to me, but I was surprised at the number of people who said they had never been to an open-casket funeral. My mortician friend had told me that many people these days don't want to take the time to mourn, so they request a fast funeral so they can get on with their life. I do understand that, but I think that for our mental and emotional health it's necessary that we go through the process of properly saying good-bye to our loved ones. The mortician also said he's had many people come back a year after attending a closed-casket funeral or an immediate cremation and ask him if the person was really in the casket. They didn't get to see them one last time and after a while wondered if it was real.

- Grieving doesn't happen in one fell swoop. It can

happen over a long period of time. Many people warned us that grief comes in waves, and they were right. There will be days, hours, moments when you will feel like your old self again — when you are happy and life is good. Then, boom, you dip down into grief and wonder if the pain will ever go away. As Roman said to me that morning I called him, "The best thing you can do is learn to ride the waves." They get less intense as time marches on, and the day will come when you won't have waves anymore.

- If you are one of those people who hate grief, emotions, and everything else that goes along with loss and you choose not to acknowledge any of it, you are doing a major disservice to your body. You can be as stoic and unfeeling as you want, but all those unacknowledged feelings will then be sitting somewhere in your body, and at some point your body is not going to want to store that heaviness for you. A dear friend of mine stoically went through the loss of both his parents without shedding one tear and later ended up having two heart attacks. Those feelings need to be dealt with and released in some way, rather than stored in the body. If you're not a crier, get as much physical exercise as you can. Help the body to release the grief.

If a Friend Is Grieving

If you're the friend of someone who is grieving and you're not sure what you can do to help, check in with them from time to time. Reassure them that you're there if they need to talk. Don't take it personally if they don't answer your calls or texts. After my mom died, many of my friends sent a short, loving text, and that was about all I could handle in the beginning. I was feeling a strong sense of loneliness, so it was good to hear from the people I love. People still sent cards and notes a month after Mom passed, and it was so nice to hear from them and know that they were still thinking of me and my family.

It has been very healing for me when people have said, "Tell me about your mom." There is nothing you can do to take away your friend's grief, but if you have time to listen, invite them to reminisce about the person they have lost. Just being able to talk about their loved one will help them to heal. The day will come when they will stop talking about them and you will be able to see in their eyes that your old friend is back.

There is no set time when it comes to grief. If your friend has lost others and never grieved those losses, it may take years for them to move through their grief. If they were like me, grieving through the whole dying process, their grief will not last as long. I know it can be very hard to be around a grieving person, but your turn will come someday and you will be grateful then to have a friend who is there for you.

Grieving on the Other Side

We aren't the only ones who suffer when someone close to us dies — the deceased person also goes through a grieving period. It will be less intense for some than for others. People who are in a longer dying process do a lot of their grieving here, so it's less intense for them when they get to the other side. But for people who die quickly, such as my friend Buck who was killed instantly, the grieving process may take a while.

Right after I got the call about his accident I checked in on his soul, expecting to find him on the other side, but Buck was still on this side with his two children. He was sitting with his wife and family while they were all discussing this horrendous loss. His wife was in a deep state of grief and shock, and he was terribly worried about her. He didn't know if she would be able to get through this, so he stayed on this side for a few weeks before going over to the other side. He was with her constantly, trying to talk to her and reassure her that he was there with her.

I tried talking to Buck, but he had put up a wall around himself because he was overwhelmed and could only handle so much at a time. He was in deep grief for his lost life and was deeply concerned for his wife and two remaining children. He did eventually go to the other side when he knew that his wife had turned a corner and would be okay. He was also very concerned about his oldest daughter because when she was in the hospital with broken bones, they discovered she had cancer! The doctors said that if this accident hadn't occurred they probably wouldn't have discovered the cancer until it was too late. The accident actually saved her life.

When Buck finally went on to the other side, he got help for his own grief and is finally, a year later, doing much better. He now sees a strength in his wife that wouldn't have formed if the accident hadn't occurred. He would still rather be here with her and his other two children, but instead of being regretful, he has found peace with his death.

✵

Whether we're here on this side of the veil or on the other side, we all find ways to cope with loss. Heaven's got just as many caregivers as we have here, so no one is without help. *How it goes is really up to us.* We can stay stuck in the tragedy of loss, or we can find some measure of good in it. Sometimes it takes a while, but if we focus on looking for the good in our loss, we find it much more quickly. That holds true on both sides of the veil.

Conclusion

$\mathcal{S}$ome deaths are hard and painful, while other deaths are easy and pain-free. The pain that death brings to the living is wrenching and debilitating, but at times death brings relief and joy because we know that our deceased loved one is no longer suffering. My sense is that we dread death because we don't talk about it, we don't understand it, and we have a lot of religious misconceptions that keep us from knowing the truth about it. We also have the incorrect idea that it is final.

I hope that this book has helped you see death in a different light. Yes, it's hard and it sucks (that's right — I said "sucks"), but we can get through it and we do carry on when we lose a loved one.

If you are the one about to make your journey home to the other side, I want to remind you that there is a reason why you are leaving and your loved ones are staying here. They will find a way to live without you. Losing you is part of their life plan, just as finishing up things here and heading home is part of your life plan.

And if you are the one left here on earth, mourning the loss of a loved one, know that the pain from loss fades a little bit as each day passes — *if you let it*. Go through your grieving process and remind yourself daily that there are reasons why you are meant to live without this person. Look for the good. It makes me smile to think that my mom died while I was finishing up this book. It's as though she wanted to help me by giving me the experience of losing her and the understanding that our continued communication has given me.

Ask the universe to help you see the bigger picture. Don't pull on the energy of the person you've lost, because they are going through a transition just as you are and aren't in a position to comfort you. Instead, reach out to friends, family, and your higher power. If you're asking for the right things — direction, guidance, comfort, and help — your answers and support will come.

I wish you nothing but the best that life — and death — has to offer as you travel down your path.

God bless,
Echo

Acknowledgments

Thanks always to my dear editor Yvette Bozzini, who made writing this book a pleasure.

Thanks to my totally cool publisher, New World Library — particularly Editorial Director Georgia Hughes, who has the patience of a saint; Managing Editor Kristen Cashman, who turned my manuscript into a book; and Senior Publicist Kim Corbin, who will now work her magic to get this book out into the world.

To all the clients and friends who have trusted me to be a part of their dying process, I thank you from the bottom of my heart. It's because of your experiences that I have been able to write this book and share this information with the world.

And, always, thanks to my family, the Bodines.

About the Author

*E*cho Bodine is a renowned spiritual healer, psychic, and teacher. She has written eleven books, including *Echoes of the Soul, The Gift, Hands That Heal, The Little Book of True Ghost Stories, Look for the Good and You'll Find God, My Big Book of Healing*, and *A Still, Small Voice*. She lectures throughout the country on intuition, spiritual healing, life, death, and life after death. She also offers workshops through The Center, her teaching and healing center in Minneapolis, Minnesota. She can be reached at:

echo@echobodine.com

or

PO Box 19488
Minneapolis, MN 55419